A Confusion of Congues

Paul Revere Frothingham

BIBLIOLIFE

A Confusion of Tongues

BY

PAUL REVERE FROTHINGHAM

BOSTON AND NEW YORK

HOUGHTON MIFFLIN COMPANY

The Riverside Press Cambridge

1917

Contents

A Confusion of Tongues

INTRODUCTION

INTRODUCTION

WE have been living in a new and unfamiliar world since August 1914. A great gulf is fixed between the things that were thought and done before that date and those which have been thought and undertaken since. Moreover, what has come to pass is destined to remain essentially unchanged for the rest of our days. Henceforth we are doomed — those of us who have reached maturity or middle-age — to read of war and, more or less constantly, to think of war so long as we have eyes and minds with which to read and think at all.

The War itself, of course, will come to an end — in time: but not so the thoughts which have been aroused, the burdens which have been incurred, the sadness which has been experienced, the doubts which have been awakened. These have come to stay, whether for better or for worse, whether to guide us or confuse. And yet, in most respects, of course, the world remains the same. It could not well be otherwise; for human duties and desires are eternal, while the deep things of the soul abide unchanged through convulsions, catastrophes, and unprecedented losses. In other words, although the world is in confusion, individual conduct and the principles which make all conduct beautiful and good, survive unshaken and have suffered no eclipse.

It is of these unshaken things a recent writer[1] speaks when he says: "We shall hear no more of the little cults that

[1] A. G. Gardiner, *The War Lords*.

used to amuse us with their affectations of gravity. They have gone in the general conflagration. Henceforth we shall be concerned not about the decorations of life, but about its foundations. . . . For the world has gone to a school that will change all its scheme of values." Of these "foundations of life" it is always profitable to think ; but never more so than in the present moment. While hundreds of thousands of people in other and older lands are suffering bravely, and enduring heroically, and dying cheerfully for what they hold to be the right, it is for us, in a land where peace is not without its perplexities, to live, so far as is possible, earnestly, unselfishly, hopefully, and well.

The chapters that follow in this little book do not deal directly with the Great War, nor do they discuss its problems ;

but they all reflect, in some measure, its terrifying glare, and none of them would be the same except for the colossal tragedy across the sea. In themselves, the separate and more or less disjointed essays represent an attempt to ease a little the present mental strain, to restore the confidence of people, and to lead the mind back to the everlasting verities of life and duty. Christopher Benson has well said: "We cannot at this time disengage our thoughts from the War: we cannot and we ought not. Still less can we take refuge from it in idle dreams of peace and security. But, at a time when every book and paper that we see is full of the War and its sufferings, there must be men and women who would do well to turn their hearts and minds a little way from it, and to let their spirits have a wider range."

Introduction

Such is the purpose of this brief volume, and with this intent it is offered to the public. Its message and its plea are a reminder that, "though worlds may crash and fall about us, the Cross endures."

Chapter One

A CONFUSION OF TONGUES

A CONFUSION OF TONGUES

THE story of the Tower of Babel is familiar. It has come of late to have a new significance. The War has found its way to the neighborhood of the scene which gave the legend birth. For, near the site of ancient Babylon and not far from Kut-el-Amarah, there still may be seen, so we are told,[1] a gigantic ruin. A shapeless mass, it lifts itself above the desert sands, serving for miles around as a landmark watched for by native shepherds and nomad merchants.

That ruin is all that remains of an ancient temple once dedicated to the great god *Bel*. Originally it was one of the most

[1] *The Bible for Learners*, vol. I, p. 89.

enormous and magnificent buildings of
proud and stately Babylon. Its height,
we are assured, was such that it far
exceeded the Great Pyramid of Egypt.
But, when Babylon was destroyed, this
great temple was destroyed; and thus it
came about that the Hebrews of succeeding generations saw it but a mass of
ruins. *Babel*, which signifies *God's Gate*,
they mistook for their own word, *bālal*,
which means *to confuse* or *confound*: and
they told this story of the giant structure.

The people of the old days, they said,
all spoke the same language. United
thereby, and proud in their strength, they
determined to construct a tower that
should reach to heaven. The work went
on apace. The tower rose and rose in
height until, at length, the Lord became
alarmed. Human beings must somehow be restrained. Their building was

too vast. A check must be given their ambition. So God devised this very simple plan: He set them to speaking different languages. Suddenly their speech became confused. And now the brickmakers could not understand the orders given by the masters. Those who mixed the mortar did not know what the teamsters and the hod-carriers were talking about. And thus they fell apart. Bewildered and at variance, they became separated into hostile groups and their mighty work was checked and left unfinished.

Such, according to the story, was the origin of different languages; and difference in language led to a loss of constructive power. So long as people were of one speech and understood each other, they could work together; and, working together, they built toward heaven. No sooner, however, did diversity of speech occur than they became estranged; separation followed estrangement and the task they had in hand was left to suffer and to fall into decay.

As a scientific theory, offered in explanation of a world-wide fact, this story is, of course, absolutely worthless. It is utterly without foundation. Not thus, nor in any way remotely like it, did the various languages of the world arise. We now know that language, like all things else, has grown. There never was any one, original, God-given tongue. Man's acquisition of speech was a result of his gregarious habits. Language is wholly and solely a social institution. Man speaks to impart his thoughts, and speech grew up on a basis of sounds. A solitary man never would have developed a language since the need for it never would have arisen.

Moreover, the thing that language grew

A Confusion of Tongues

out of is a thing that it promotes — and
that is social intercourse and coherency
of effort. Men who speak the same language are naturally and inevitably drawn
together and held together. The "barbarian," to a Greek, was a man who spoke
in a tongue differing from his own — a
tongue which sounded like *ba-ba* and
which he could not understand.

That old story of the Hebrews has,
therefore, an important moral lesson, and
one which bears alike upon individual
life and upon community effort. Here
were men who were working together,
doing mighty, heaven-reaching things.
But they fell apart and their work was
destroyed because they ceased to speak
a common language. No sooner, therefore, do we look upon language in its
larger bearings, as a medium for expressing thoughts, ideas, and principles of life,

than we come to see the lesson that the ancient legend has to teach us. And surely, in its far-reaching consequences, it is a lesson which has a tragic and an awful meaning for us in the present time.

It is somewhat customary to speak of people as using different languages when they simply come at things from a different avenue of approach. The language of the poor man is different from the language of the rich man. The language of the man who receives wages is different from the language of the man who pays them. Hence it is that, so frequently, such people fail to understand each other. They move in different spheres and each to the other is, in the ancient Greek sense of the word, more or less of a barbarian. It was Rabelais, whose name has come to be a synonym for the cynics and the scoffers of the race, who said long years ago, in words that are often quoted, that one half of the world knows not how the other half lives. And the reason for this lack of mutual understanding is a difference of language.

In former days it was considered a large part of education to know many languages. The scholar was—and to a large extent still is—the person who is versed in various tongues. He is the man who can speak with strangers from a foreign country; who can read Homer or the Bible in the original; who can translate the thoughts of Vergil, or understand the words of Dante. And this is well: this is a standard which must be maintained. What we have forgotten, however, or have failed to realize in full is this—that it is a part of moral education and an indication of enlightenment to do the same thing in a broader and a higher sense. In

9

the broader and the higher spheres of human 'life and effort are many languages: there is the language of the heart — the language of deep human needs; there are the differing languages that voice differing ideals, differing hopes, desires, and ambitions; and unless we can enter into, speak, translate, and understand such tongues as these, we stamp ourselves as humanly provincial and our education is most seriously defective. We do not live our lives as they might be lived and as they *should* be lived until we learn, at least in part, to understand each other, to interpret one another's needs, and to take each the other's point of view. More trouble in this world results from needless *mis*understanding than from almost any other cause. We become provoked with people, we engage in quarrels with them, sometimes we treat them harshly, and often we permit ourselves to become permanently estranged — all this simply because we have not taken pains to learn just what they wish to say and are struggling to express. In the most literal sense we fail to understand them.

And that being true in a negative sense, surely the very opposite is true when we have the gift of tongues and have learned the lesson of wide and deep and generous interpretation. The Good Samaritan — whom we call " good " because he had this precious gift — went promptly to the assistance of a wounded fellow-man : — and why? It was because he understood the language of human suffering. He was able to translate the needs of another in distress into terms of his own experience and feeling. He was able to put himself in the other's place

— to feel as he felt, to see as he saw, and to suffer as he was suffering. In the deepest sense these two understood and spoke a common tongue; and it was the tongue of what was human.

Just at present the world is suffering the calamity of the most awful war that has ever taken place in history. This War is inflicting greater loss, entailing greater suffering, causing greater agony, bringing with it greater and more complete confusion than the world, in its whole long history, has ever known before. And how has it come about? What has brought this fearful ruin to our race? We were building up, as it seemed, the tower of the proudest, and the truest, and the most complete civilization that the world had ever known. It was heaven-reaching in its high ideals and its dreams of a broad, complete humanity. But, suddenly, like the work of old in the plains of ancient Babylon, the process of construction ceased ; a confusion of tongues ensued, and a ruined tower is the sad result which future generations of the race will look upon with awe and sad misgivings.

There is little use, perhaps, in looking just at present on the causes. And yet we can hardly fail to see the most conspicuous ; for history takes up at times the tale of legend. I was re-reading in part, the other day, one of the most remarkable little books that the War has called out in America. I mean *The Pentecost of Calamity*, by Owen Wister. My readers will remember how Mr. Wister emphasizes the way in which Germany had shut herself in from the world. " Even her Socialist-Democrats conformed to military principles and teachings," he says. "China built a stone wall, but Germany a wall of the mind." For forty years she learned and repeated "Prussian incantations." And "within her wall of moral isolation," thinking only of her own aspirations, speaking only of her own hopes, desires, ambitions, her sight became distorted and her sense of proportion quite lost. When, therefore, she struck her sudden blow, she was amazed to find that the world was against her, abhorrent of the things she did. This, then, was her Nemesis: she had misunderstood the world, feeling all the while that she herself was misunderstood. It was a tragic instance of the danger that always lurks in centering your thoughts upon yourself and thinking only of your own hopes, desires, and needs. What is necessary for one's self, and for self-development, one comes to look upon as right and proper and, indeed, the only justifiable need for all. One's own language is the only language and one's own culture the culture that the world most needs.

In this respect, of course, as in many another, the nation is only the larger individual. Here, therefore, is a danger that all of us have to guard against and to learn, if possible, to counteract. The world inevitably divides itself into classes. Society is made up of different kinds of people, living under differing conditions and enjoying widely divergent degrees of opportunity and privilege. There are cultured classes and ignorant classes; there are rich and poor; there are high and low; there are head-workers and hand-workers; there are capitalists and laborers; there are conservatives and radicals; there are people of leisure and people of incessant, grinding, and poorly requited toil. And, to whichever class we may happen to belong, it is right and wise, it is proper and much to be desired that we learn, so far as is possible, to put ourselves in other people's places and to understand their language and emotions. Society progresses and builds securely, rearing its tower upon deep and firm foundations, only in proportion as people have one language and use a common speech of high and pure ideals.

A year or two ago the head worker in a well-known social settlement was speaking with reference to the chief value of all such institutions. And he did not emphasize the advantages which the social settlement offers to the children of the poor and to the family of the immigrant. He did not dwell upon the good that is done in the clubs, nor upon the instruction and refinement that, directly or indirectly, are imparted by college graduates and others to those who are ignorant of the amenities of life. Not at all. But what he did enlarge upon and emphasize was this: that the social settlement is a place where the often widely divergent classes in our American society are interpreted to one another; where they learn to speak a common language and are made to understand, in part, each other's point of view. The teacher, he said, is often taught, while the learner comes to read life in a truer light. The rich and the poor, the privileged and the handicapped, come to see things, each from the other side of the wall that outward condition has built up between them. Thus the capitalist comes to learn something of what the socialist is driving at, and the socialist is awakened to the fact that wealth and power are not always selfish, base, and overbearing.

It is true that these lessons are never easy ones to learn. All of us tend to live within our own enclosures, speaking the language which conditions, customs, education, and tradition make familiar to us. We are colored, all of us, by our surroundings, shaped by our inheritances, influenced by our privileges or the lack of them; until, at length, it comes about that prejudice usurps the place of reason and wields a sovereign, though perhaps unconscious, sway. And prejudice, you know, is neither more nor less than just *pre-judging* things before one has heard the evidence or made an effort to arrive at facts. Moreover, for us Americans, these lessons, however difficult, have special importance. For if we are to build and to keep our nation as it should be built and kept, if we would purify its politics, adjust its conflicting social interests, and encourage public spirit, civic zeal, and social service, it behooves us, to these ends, to cultivate a common speech and to learn to understand the language of hopes and dreams and interests that differ from our own. And how is this common speech to be acquired? it may be asked. Well—in spite of all those differences which never wholly can be done away, do we not all know this: that there *is* a sphere in which, like those of old, we have one language and employ one speech? That sphere is the higher sphere where ideals reign and principles are upheld and standards are defended. Let us seek example of this truth.

As I write, the footfalls of the various great Preparedness Parades have hardly died away. The thought of those moving columns is still before our minds and we needs must ask ourselves, What is it that they symbolize? What is the true significance of this movement for Preparedness, with all its great dimensions and its power of spectacular display? For what does it *prepare* the way? At present, I confess, it seems crude and noisy; at present it has elements that waken doubt and make us feel that in more than one direction it may reach too far. But, in spite of this, the Preparedness propaganda appeals to me as containing the elements of great and liberal promise. For Preparedness is a means and not an end; it is a messenger that goes before the face of larger things and literally prepares the way for a dispensation that has long been looked for in a country where, of late years, we have had too little of the patriotism which is

built upon service and imbued with the
spirit of self-sacrifice. All too frequently,
of late, people have come to our country, and people have grown up in our
country, not with the spirit of giving,
but of getting; not with the thought of
what they could do for America, but of
what America could do for them. Hence
graft has grown; hence civic selfishness
has grown; hence careless indolence as
regards the public weal has grown.
Rights, not duties, have been emphasized; selfish gain, not public service;
the promotion of financial schemes rather
than the promotion of our country's good.
What I like about this movement for
Preparedness is the emphasis it lays upon
the need of a common service and a mutual understanding.

These camps that are being organized,
these multiple organizations that are be-

ing formed, these groups of all kinds
that are being drawn together, to work
together, to march together, to serve together, — they are all helping toward the
acquisition of a common tongue for common needs. They are all combining to
prepare the way for a closer social unity
and a finer understanding of Democracy.
For they bring people of all kinds together and thus do away with false dis-
tinctions; they remove all petty barriers
and thus are able to fire great masses of
the people with the sense of a common
purpose and a common obligation.

And when we set ourselves to build
on such foundations, — be our structure
city, state, or nation, — then indeed we
build toward heaven; then our diver-
gences of speech become forgotten; we
understand each other and we help each
other. And then a Higher Power com-

ing down, neither confuses nor scatters us. But He sees the tower that is building to be his own — a Temple of the Spirit; and henceforth God and man are laborers together, speaking and understanding the language of the Spirit.

Chapter Two

THE CONDUCT OF LIFE

THE CONDUCT OF LIFE

IF there is one thing emphasized more than any other in our Bible, that thing is *Life*. The Bible, indeed, is not so much a Book of Law as a Book of Life. It does not deal with maxims half so much as it deals with men. It is not concerned with codes half so much as it is with conduct. Man is the Bible's first interest; and man as his life relates itself to God and to his fellow-men.

Moreover, what is true of the Bible as a whole, is more particularly true of that portion of the Book which contains the teaching of the Master. The great word of Jesus, the word which He used more frequently and more earnestly than any

27

other, was the one word *Life*. "I," He said of Himself, "I am the bread of Life." "I am the Way, the Truth, and the Life." To the wondering woman who stood with Him at the well in Samaria He said, "Whoso drinketh of this water shall thirst again; but the water that I shall give him shall be in him a well of water, springing up into eternal life." Again He could say, "I am come that they might have life, and that they might have it more abundantly"; adding also, in another connection, "He that findeth his life shall lose it; and he that loseth his life shall find it." All of this, of course, is most familiar. But what is somewhat less familiar is the thought that the reward of all right living, according to this same supremely spiritual Teacher, is still in terms of *Life*. "This do, and thou shalt have" — not luxuries, nor ease, nor wealth, nor honor, nor any outward earthly thing; but, "This do and thou shalt *live.*"

Now, in these days, when Death is playing a larger and more conspicuous part in the great drama of events than ever before in the history of the world; when, accordingly, there is so much to perplex us, and disturb us, and depress us, I have a feeling that it may be well and wise and helpful to center our thoughts, so far as is possible, upon subjects which are connected with the conduct of *life.* And just because world-events have loomed so large, and the problems of national and international existence have become so gigantic and insistent and disturbing; just because we are forced to think, as never until now, of destiny and duty, of suffering, loss, and sorrow in the large, I feel that there is wisdom in getting back to the thought of things that are ever with us, and in seeking new light upon the ever-present problems of *individual* existence. For, no matter how disturbed the world may be, nor how dark the sky, nor how draped with clouds the far horizon, each one of us has still his little life to live, and all of us desire to live as well as possible. To that end we should strive to discover what it is that we must do if we would have the " more abundant life " of which the Master spoke.

One of the most interesting men of a previous generation in New England was Emerson's friend and neighbor, Bronson Alcott. Some one has said that the chief benefit he conferred upon the world was in giving to it his talented and brilliant daughter. But Alcott, with all his eccentricities and vague endeavors for reform, saw clearly enough along certain lines — especially those of education. Upon one occasion, we are told, he went into a school at Concord. Being asked to say something to the children, he stood up, looked at them for a time, and then asked abruptly, "What do you come here for?" The inevitable and familiar period of silence and embarrassment ensued. But the questioner persisted and, at last, one pupil, bolder than the rest, replied that they came to learn. "Yes," persisted the philosopher, "but to learn what?" Finally came the answer he desired: "To learn how to behave." And is not this the thing we are all engaged in learning in the greater school of the world, with whatever days and weeks, with whatever months and years are granted to us? We are not solving many problems; we are not dispelling many mysteries; but, whether successfully or unsuccessfully, whether completely or only partially, under varying circumstances, face to face with perplexities and privileges, with pleasures and sorrows, opportunities and trials, we are all engaged in learning how to conduct ourselves — which is to say, how to behave.

If I wished, therefore, I could stop right here and devote an entire essay to that single word, *Behave*. It would be rather more of a sermon than an essay. Indeed, one of the world's great sermons, contained in Dr. Martineau's precious volume, *Endeavours after the Christian Life*, bears the title *Having, Doing, Being*. It is a sermon, in the highest sense, upon Behavior.

Let us split apart that word *be-have*. It is plainly seen to be compounded of two of the commonest, yet most significant, words in the English language. Taken in conjunction with each other, these words involve some of the most persistent difficulties that exist for us in this life. To *be* and to *have*: — to *be* simple, let us say, while we *have* wealth and all that wealth lays down at our feet; to *be* patient and cheerful, while we *have* troubles, disappointments, and trials; these are tasks which forever present themselves to the individual life; while, just at present, we are called upon as a nation to *be* trustful and believing, while we *have* for outlook the evil of the world, rolled up until the entire sky of life is dark.

Confronted by problems such as these, all of us need and desire information. And I have often had the feeling that it would be most convenient and satisfactory if only there were in life some such bureau or department as we find in any modern railway station of size or importance. Life is a journey. It has destinations that we wish to reach. And sometimes — very often, indeed — we are puzzled as to the best, the safest, and the quickest line by which to travel. Under such circumstances, in a railway station, we consult an office which is set apart for "Information." He we find some one whose function is to help and guide all travelers. We ask our questions and they are answered for us — answered with authority by an official whose business it is to know. That settles the matter; and if, afterwards, mistakes are made, the fault is with ourselves.

Sometimes, however, our puzzles are of a deeper and a darker kind, and not thus easily disposed of. They involve the mazes and the intricacies of our very inmost natures and desires. And when we find ourselves entangled in a network of such character, it has been suggested [1] that a method not unlike the one employed at Hampton Court might prove of value. In the park of that picturesque old Palace there is a famous maze which affords perennial interest and delight for visitors. A labyrinth of winding walks has been arranged between high hedges. It is easy enough to enter this labyrinth, but most difficult, once in, to find a way that brings one out. It is impossible to see any point of egress, or to discover whither the intricate paths are reaching. At Hampton Court, therefore, a man has been stationed "on a little platform, just outside the maze and just above it." And when one has become hopelessly involved, and

[1] Stephen Paget, *The New Parent's Assistant*, p. 6.

is tired of taking useless turns, and of wandering round and round, appeal is made to this man upon the platform. Following his directions one easily finds the way and is soon — sometimes very suddenly — released. No one thinks of doubting or of contradicting the director, " for he is outside and above the maze," and sees where no other can.

In similar fashion, involved in the maze of life, we may all of us turn to those great teachers and wise guides whose range of vision is so much wider and more lofty than our own. In the present connection, therefore, let us turn to the wisest guide and supremest teacher of them all. Let us consider what he had to say. "This do," was his word to the lawyer who questioned as to the right conduct of life — "This do, and thou shalt live." And the first rule he gave, and the great rule, was the simple one of kindness. Would you live well? Be kind. Would you live rightly and completely? Be considerate and helpful. This was his word to those about him — the word which, above all others, has come down across the centuries. And I wonder, for my own part, whether, as a matter of very actual and evident fact, there is anything that counts for more in life, the memory of which lasts longer and more blessedly, than just that simple quality of heart. Courage is a strong quality; perseverance is a useful quality; integrity is fundamental and we cannot do without it; but kindness has the beauty of inherent usefulness, together with the gentleness that is born of strength.

"Go back," says a writer [1] whose words I was reading but the other day, "Go

[1] George A. Gordon, *Through Man to God*, p. 199.

back into the fair morning of your life; recall the time when the world was new, when everything came to you in the mystery of fresh experience; and ask the question — Who were they that interested and delighted you most in that golden age?" And then: "Personally," he adds, "I have done that a hundred times; I have gone back into the morning of life, and looked again upon the men and women who then compassed me about. There were men and women saintly, truly so: and I regret to say that I did not like the saints. There were the men of courage, and they were better. Then came the patriots . . . who filled my mind with inspiring tales. But, high above all the persons of that early period, are the kind people. I can see them at the far end of a long vista, with the light of God shining in their faces. There they

38

remain in that silent world, images of beauty and humanity, wearing looks that then seemed, and that still seem, the best symbol of heaven: playmates, some of them, forever vanished and yet unforgettable; dear old mothers and grandmothers, who were fascinating simply because of their unwearying kindness."

This testimony of another would be, I believe, the testimony likewise of nearly all of us. There is no influence so potent to guide and keep and bless us through the eager, stormy years of youth, in the busy toil and restless energy of middle man- or womanhood, and on "until the shadows lengthen, and the evening comes, and the busy world is hushed, and the fever of life is over, and our work is done"; there is nothing that abides so long, or stands out with such clearness, as the grace of kindness.

And what is kindness? — a word which, to my mind, is in many ways a greater word than love, and a more helpful word than sympathy. What is kindness in its deepest nature and its widening reaches, if not a simple sense of other people, and of all people, as belonging with ourselves to the same great kin, or *kind*. We are kind when we are human and recognize the humanity that is in others. Not all of us have that human sense in any marked degree of development to begin with; not all of us are naturally considerate and thoughtful. But all of us have the power, if we wish to use it, of developing the sense and quickening the impulses of which it is composed. And for our own good, as well as for the good of others, I can think of no one quality which counts for more, when well developed and rightly exercised. It counts toward the rightful doing of our work; and it counts not less, but rather more, toward the building of God's kingdom. I remember to have heard, not long ago, of a man who was looked upon as disqualified for a post of great importance, for the simple reason that he lacked this quality. The position in question involved the management of men and the employment of labor upon one of our New England railways. And this man had ability, he had energy, he had resources. But, because he lacked the human sense and felt no kinship with the toilers of the world, he was judged — and rightly judged — to be unfitted for such post. He was the sort of man who talks of factory "hands," and looks at "labor" in the mass, forgetful of the fact that behind the hands are hearts and consciences, and that the labor problem has to do with men and women and with children who live together and establish homes.

Had there been more kindness in the world — a keener sense, that is, of the *kin*ship of the peoples of all nations — there would be no war in Europe at the present time. Men fall apart and fight each other when they forget about the things which make them, and should keep them, *one*.

In large ways, therefore, as in little ones, this quality should be looked on as supreme in considering the rightful conduct of our lives. It is, indeed, a " Golden Rule " — always to be thought of and safely to be acted on: " This do and thou shalt live."

It is significant, I think, that, if we look at the life and character of one of the greatest among modern men, we shall find this the trait that was conspicuous above all others in his lifetime and that is recalled most frequently by all who reflect upon his character and career. The greatness of Abraham Lincoln was in large part due to the greatness of his heart. It will evermore remain among the anomalies of history, as also a tragedy of human destiny, that one of the fiercest and most bloody wars which the world has ever known was conducted by one of the tenderest and most humane men that ever lived. No section of the country could secede from him or forfeit finally the right to his forgiveness and forbearance. No State could successfully rebel against his earnest and untiring wish to heal the breach that so unfortunately had been made. Through the long and fearful period of struggle, when hatred of the fiercest sort had been engendered, he held that all the people had a rightful claim upon his sympathies, and that wayward citizens, like erring children, should be lured and welcomed back into the fold. All sorrows were his sorrows: all burdens, whether at the North or South, seemed his to bear. Though hated and harassed, though tried and tempted beyond measure, — how significant it is that not one word of malice or of rancor, not a phrase which, after the cessation of hostilities, might return to embitter the defeated combatants or to be resented by their descendants, could be remembered of him. The thing that *is* remembered, and that will never be forgotten, is the immortal sentence that he wrote and that gives a guiding principle for the conduct of his life: " With malice toward none, with charity for all; with firmness in the right as God gives us to see the right, let us strive on to finish the work we are in; to bind up this Nation's wounds; to do all which may achieve and cherish a just and lasting peace."

"With malice toward none, with charity for all" — I can think of no better rule than that for the rightful conduct of life, whether it be the life of an individual or of a nation. It is the rule of simple kindness. When we are perplexed and weary, when we are injured or offended, when we are angry, envious, or distrustful, when we are lost in the maze of life and seek for guidance, let us recall that rule as given by one who stood outside of life, and above it, in the exaltation of his soul.

But there was a second thing that the lawyer in old Jerusalem was reminded of as necessary if he really wished to live. It stood *first* in the ancient Book of the Law. Men spoke of it then — and it still is spoken of — as " Loving God." But, for my own part, I prefer to think of it, at least in this connection, as Reverence. And what I wish to say, with neither argument nor illustration, is simply this: if kindness is the first thing necessary for the rightful conduct of life, then reverence is easily the second. Beware of the man — beware especially of the woman — who reverences nothing; to whom life offers nothing by which the knee instinctively is bent, the soul suffused with awe, and the mind transfigured with the sense of wonder.

Andrew Jackson, we are told, uncouth and ill-mannered though he was, once remarked to his friend, Francis Blair, that Aaron Burr had come " within one trait of the most exalted greatness. ' What was that?' asked Mr. Blair. 'Reverence, sir, reverence,' replied the General solemnly. 'I don't care how smart, or how highly educated, or how widely experienced a man may be in this world's affairs; unless he reverences something, and believes in something beyond his own self, he will fall short somewhere. That was the trouble with Burr. I saw it when I first met him in 1796. I was a raw backwoodsman, but I never could get over that one impression that he was irreverent. I remember reading away back yonder how he said, when he read Hamilton's farewell letter, that it sounded like the confession of a penitent monk. I thought then, Blair, that if I had killed a man as he killed Hamilton, I would have left that for some one else to say. Yes: a man must revere something; or, no matter how smart or brave he is, he will die as Burr died in New York the other day, friendless and alone.'"

It is true that, without this element of which General Jackson spoke so understandingly, our lives lack the human and escape the holy. We may not have deep beliefs or firm convictions to guide us on our journey; but what man is he who does not recognize somewhere a Power Higher than himself? In this world, with its immeasurable distances and its mighty depths; with its laws that make for beauty, and its lines that go out through all the earth; where the heavens declare the glory of God and human beings find nothing that comforts and contents them like the good, we needs must acknowledge something that commands our reverence and worship. And by such acknowledgment we all are lifted up. Indeed, it may be said that he alone conducts his life aright who feels that somehow, and in ways beyond his knowledge, he is led and guided from on high.

For we know in part, and we only prophesy in part; and, until the perfect is attained, it is just for us to go upon our way with reverence for what is holy, and devotion to the law of right.

Chapter Three

A MOTTO

A MOTTO

In the twelfth century of our era there lived in France a certain scholar — Alain de Lille — otherwise known as *Alanus ab Insulis*. He was a monk of the Cistercian order and his learning was such that he came to be known throughout mediæval Europe as the *Universal Doctor*. As a monk he had given his heart to God. As a scholar he had given his mind to learning. And, doubtless as expressing the essence and deep motive of his long career, he formulated this motto: "Live as if you were to die to-morrow: Learn as if you were to live forever."

If we study this motto we shall find

that it covers those two great realms or departments of human existence which forever stand related to and bear incessantly upon each other. At times the first appears supreme; and then the second rises up for recognition. Now one is given emphasis, and now the other. But they never can be separated; for the two belong together and together form the sum and substance of all being. Within these two complementary spheres are included life and learning; virtue and knowledge; action and impulse; duty and dream; conduct and creed; practice and theory; behavior and belief; character and conviction. And these opposites, in each case, form one whole. They never can be looked upon as independent of each other. For life should be enriched as far as possible by learning; duty depends upon the dream that lies behind it; creed is impotent divorced from conduct; while theory waits for practice to make it good and beautiful and true. What that mediæval monk whose mind was filled with learning says to us is this: that in the first of life's departments we should look at what is near; in the second we should fling our gaze afar; that in living we should live from day to day; while in learning we should take long views of things and fix our gaze upon that which lies at the end of the vista. The *here* of duty, and the *there* of glowing visions and ideals: the *now* of conduct, and the long, unmeasured, and uncounted years for progress and development—these are his themes. Let us give some thought to these themes and endeavor to relate them to the sphere of everyday life and conduct.

We will begin with the first injunction: "Live as if you were to die to-morrow." Now there are those, I know, who start back in revolt from such a precept. Why should we live, they say, forever conscious of the sad, unwelcome fact that life must have an end; that existence is as fleeting as the shadow; that we are here to-day, and to-morrow the places that we occupied are vacant. This is the old, melancholy, and much mistaken attitude toward things. It should be outgrown: it has been outgrown. It belongs to ignorant and superstitious times, when death was feared and was carefully prepared for because of the punishment that might await men in the great hereafter. It recalls the ominous and warning words of old: "In the midst of life we are in death: What is your life: it is even as a vapour that appeareth for a little time and vanisheth away." We hear again the sharp cry of the Great Apostle: "Brethren, the time is short: now is our salvation nearer than when we first believed." Yes; and it may be that the suggestion carries us still further and we find ourselves in contemplation of those mediæval pictures, sometimes called the *Dance of Death*, in which the figure of Death is represented meeting the merchant as he counts his gold; lying in wait for the mechanic as he goes out to his work; smiting the musician as he gayly plays at some great feast.

No — No — we have said. Let not our lives be shadowed thus, as the lives of men were darkened in the days of old. " Live as if you were to die to-morrow ": — that is the motto of a grim old monk who believed that sadness was a duty, and the world an evil, and that men should give their thoughts, not to the here and now, but to the vast hereafter. Consequently, in our reaction, we have gone to the very opposite extreme. There are those who live as if they were to live forever in this world; who banish not alone all talk, but, so far as possible, all thought of death; who lay no plans, give no directions, make no wills. Such as these, when they are gone, leave their affairs in great confusion. They too are victims, in another way, of superstition.

But between these two extremes, which are neither of them to be commended, it appears to me that we can find a large and middle ground which all of us should occupy. The facts of life can never, any of them, wisely be avoided. The fact of death should be accepted by us all and used for the right and wise development of life. It is not something to be feared, but it *is* something to be faced. And when we face it as a simple fact it has many a lesson it can teach us, many an impulse it can give toward what is right and true, unselfish, pure, and holy.

Live as though the span of life extended for us only through a brief to-morrow — suppose that any of us did that; suppose that we made a principle of doing it; what probable effect would it have upon our actions? Would it make us sad, indifferent, and inactive? Would it impel us to leave our tasks undone, our efforts incomplete, our duties hopelessly neglected? Would it persuade us that nothing after all was much worth while; that it was just as well to let things take their course? I do not think so. Quite the contrary. It seems to me that such a thought would lend a form of deep intensity to life. It would mean the shaking-off of miserable lethargy; the counting of the precious golden moments as they fly; the doing promptly of our duties as one by one they present themselves; and the glad acceptance of such opportunities for light and joy and service as are offered us. Phillips Brooks once said: "It is when the brook begins to hear the mighty river calling to it, and knows that its time is short, that it begins to hurry over the rocks and toss the foam in air and make straight for the valley. Life that never thinks of its end lives in the present and loses the flow and movement of responsibility. It is not so much that the shortness of life makes us prepare for death, as it is that it spreads the feeling of privilege through life and makes each moment prepare for the next — makes life prepare for life."

A Motto

I went along the street only yesterday with a man whose years have almost reached a full fourscore. It was bleak and wet and disagreeable, and I asked him if he were not tired of the winter. "Tired of the winter? Indeed, no," he answered blithely; "the more of it the better. Whether summer or winter, every day of life that is granted me I now count as a happiness and a privilege." That was the viewpoint of one who knew that the time was short.

But it seems to me that the thought of which we are speaking does more than that. It not merely adds a kind of energy and intensity to life: it leads us likewise to set the house of life in order. And I do not speak solely in regard to outward and financial things although, of course, that also would be true. In the old days of precise and methodical business men and methods, it used to be a kind of religious ideal for the merchant to balance his books carefully every night and to leave his office as though he never might return. Everything was ordered: everything prepared. It is, however, a different kind of order that I am thinking of at present—a different and a higher kind. I am thinking of the quarrels that would be ended, of the misunderstandings that would be done away, of the jealousies that would seem so poor a bequest to leave behind and that all of us would banish if we really knew that the time we had was short. Most of us mean, sometime, to forgive an actual or imaginary injury or insult; we mean, sometime, to reach out a friendly hand or to do a generous deed to some one whom we have not liked or with whom we have not been on cordial terms. And how quickly we would do it; how gladly we would welcome the opportunity to do it; how eagerly we would speak the helpful, friendly word, if we felt or knew that either he or she or we would soon have done forever with the things of earth. When we keep the precept of that old Cistercian monk in mind we do not dawdle with amiable plans, or play with good intentions; but we act — and act at once — before, perchance, it is too late.

Horace Mann, whom we honor as a prophet of the higher education, once remarked, with his usual insight and discernment, that we are told nothing in the Bible about the *resolutions* of the Apostles, or about the *plans* and *dreams* of the Apostles: we are told only about the *Acts* of the Apostles. And acts are things to which all of us would devote more ardent energies if, like the Apostles, we should come to be persuaded that the time is short. There is a sense, therefore, in which we might do well if we were to look upon ourselves as just day laborers — not working by the piece and not under any contract for a long term of years; but just given a work to do from day to day, and with strength sufficient to undertake and complete it.

" Live as if you were to die to-morrow: Learn as if you were to live forever." What shall we say with reference to the second — the larger, higher, and more welcome portion of the precept — "Learn as if you were to live forever"? As we hold in mind this injunction and relate to it all the richness and the wealth and the glow of human hopes and dreams, ambitions and ideals, it seems to lend to life a certain dignity and majesty and might. If there are ways in which we

ought to live but from day to day, taking short views of things, just as surely
there are many other ways in which we
ought to place our confidence and trust
in things that reach through time and to
eternity. There are many ways of life
and many works of life that never would
be entered on and calmly, bravely, and
hopefully undertaken, except it were
possible for mind and soul to reach out
and to dare look on through the years,
taking no thought for the immediate,
seeing no end to effort. It is thus that
the young man enters on his course of
preparation for some great profession;
it is thus that the student sets himself
to the task of long investigation; it is
thus that the scholar outlines in his
early or, it may be, in his later years,
some task that he will do. He does not
say, "It may be that I shall not live to

engage in practice; it may be that my research never will result in any discovery; it may be that my book never will be completed; therefore, why should I delve and study and perfect myself with care? It is not worth while. I will live only for to-day. I will learn only what has immediate and near-by value." No; he does not say or think such things as these. He takes no foolish thought for such a paltry thing as time. But the work is there, the strength is here; the vision is beyond, the purpose is within; the ideal beckons, and resolution rises up from silent depths of which he hardly knows the meaning. Solemnly, unconsciously, he gives himself to that which has a value he knows not how to measure, and possibilities of which he cannot see the end.

It is thus that all great work is done.

A Motto

It is thus that all great souls have always taken up and carried on the noblest tasks of life. The thought of the Eternal, the instinct of the Eternal, the purpose of the Eternal — although we hardly know it at the time — forever enter into feeble, fleeting, and inconstant human beings, and they give themselves with power and persistency to what is noble and sublime. In more ways than we know about or understand, we show ourselves and prove ourselves the children of a Higher Power and a Power that is timeless. In our work as well as in our worship, we say incessantly to somewhat that is other than ourselves, " What is thine is ours also, if we are thine: and life is eternal, and love is immortal, and death is only an horizon, and an horizon is nothing save the limit of our seeing "; and saying, we know that we can see and measure but a very little of the wonders and the possibilities by which we are surrounded. The human being is an onward-moving and an upward-reaching creature. His hopes are boundless, his dreams are unconfined; and he lives his life completely only when he lives for things which have a value in themselves, and of which he knows himself to form but a tiny and a temporary part.

Does it ever occur to us, I wonder, to consider how it is that victory was always represented by the ancients; why it was that she was always shaped and pictured as we see her in the famous statues? The old Greeks did not hew the marble from their hills to depict for men a seated victory, with folded wings, and in the posture of repose. They did not make her wear the features of contentment, nor permit her to hold the attitude of one who has attained. No; she is represented always as a figure instinct with energy, with wings outspread, and garments flowing. She moves in triumph forward, on feet that tread the air. That is the famous *Winged Victory* of the Louvre and likewise the figure that men go to old Olympia to admire. Victory is always going forward, always moving on toward things which lie beyond. It is not a question of to-day, nor yet to-morrow,—but of far ideals. And wings are things to fly with, by which we are borne upward toward the heights.

Thus it is that the only lasting victories of life are won. They come to those who reach out, and who seek the things that lie beyond. "Learn as if you were to live forever." Yes; learn and live the things that have eternal value — that are the same yesterday, to-day, and to-morrow. Learn goodness, learn mercy, learn justice, learn sympathy, learn reverence, learn truth: and learn them not for any value that they have to-day, nor for any profit they may yield in peace and happiness and service. But learn them and lay hold upon them because, whether living or dying, whether failing or succeeding, whether in this world or the next world, whether to-day or through the long to-morrow, they have enduring and eternal value.

Chapter Four

THE LITTLE BOOK

THE LITTLE BOOK

I‍N the Book of Revelation there is an account of a colossal angel. His figure filled the heaven and for support he needed both the earth and sea. The visionary Bible writer, in describing what he saw, declared that this mighty figure wore the rainbow for a crown, while his face was like the sun. When he came down from the sky and sought a place on which to stand, we are told he set his right foot on the sea and his left foot on the land. And he cried with a great voice, as a lion when it roareth.

For all his enormous size, however, the really significant thing about this mighty angel of the Revelation was the object which he held within his hand. That object was a little book. More than once we are told that the book was *little* — so small, indeed, that the Prophet was directed to take and eat it. And yet, in that book was everything written: for it was the book of the prophecy of life.

Mankind has ever had a peculiar fondness for things that are "big." The *Seven Wonders of the World* included the Pyramids of Egypt and the Colossus of Rhodes. They ranged from the Hanging Gardens of Babylon to the Great Wall of China. With one or two exceptions, however, these "wonders" — which were so different — had a single element in common: and that element was vastness. They were like the angel in the Book of Revelation, who stood with one foot on the land and the other on the sea.

In more than one respect we all are children of the ancients; and, among other things, we have inherited their love for bigness. Particularly is this true of us Americans. There is nothing of which we boast more frequently than concerning the size of the continent which we possess. We rejoice in our teeming cities, and our sweeping prairies, and our mighty rivers. The objects of our most genuine interest, it is often said, are the objects which are big — like Niagara, and the Grand Canyon, and the Big Trees of California, and the lofty peaks of the Rocky Mountains. As a people we coined the phrase " Big Business," and one phase of " Big Business " is the " Giant Trust." And there is no period of our history of which this is more truly typical than the moment in which we now live. For there is nothing of which we hear so much or that inspires such excessive confidence as "Big Guns" and "Super-Dreadnaughts."

While all of this is true, however, it is only half the truth. While, apparently, we put our trust in bigness, the real fact is that our age has emphasized, as no other age has ever done, the importance of little things and the significance of what is infinitely small. We see with the eyes of the ancient Prophet an enormous angel which fills the sky; but we see, also, that within his hand the angel bears a little book. The *biggest* discovery of recent times has been the discovery of bacteria — forms of life so tiny that only the most powerful microscope reveals them. We have dug a huge canal which unites two oceans; but we were able to do the work successfully only after we had discovered the poison-bearing power of a tiny insect — the mosquito. And finally, it remained for an American to receive the other day a prize of forty thousand dollars for learning how to weigh something. That something was not mountains, nor continents, nor planets: Professor Richards received the Nobel prize in chemistry for success in weighing *atoms*.

When we reflect upon things like these we begin to understand what a well-known English author, a prophet of the paradoxical, had in mind when he wrote, not long ago, a book he called *Tremendous Trifles*. But it needs no Gilbert Chesterton to remind us that

"The trifles of our daily lives,
    The common things scarce worth recall,
Whereof no visible trace remains; —
    These are the mainspring after all."

To some these trifles may seem relatively of no importance. Undoubtedly they constitute the lesser questions of the present day. In this boundless world, however, with its sweeping planets and its age-long currents, its vast foam eddies and its tides that ebb and flow through time and to eternity, there is nothing of which it can be safely said that "it does not matter much," or that "after all, it makes no difference."

And this is true whether in the world of natural forces or of forces that shape character; whether in nature or in life. "There is no difference," says a modern philosopher, writing on the everlasting problems of the world and God and Duty, "there is no difference worth discussing which does not make a difference in conduct"—which is to say, a difference in character, in life itself. The secret sin, if it be not corrected and crushed out, becomes in time the besetting sin which cuts into the bright career and brings it to destruction. And the same law works in nature. " 'Let that worm alone, and it will kill your tree,' was said to the gardener in the park of a great estate in England. And true enough; the gardener paid no attention to the tiny borer, and next year's yellow leaves showed the slow assassination of the tree."

Perhaps the greatest natural marvel of our continent, and it may be of the world, is the Grand Canyon of Arizona. And the difference between this yawning chasm, awakening awe with its tremendous measurements, thrilling the sensibilities with the rainbow beauty of its colorings,——the difference between the giant cliffs and the awful depths, and the dry and dreary, sun-baked level plain surrounding, is a difference due to the cumulative action of little drops of water. The brightly colored angel which here rears its head into the clouds has in its hand a little book: and in that book is written the long and secret history of the thing men travel miles to see.

But the world is full of little books. Beelzebub is the well-known Father of Lies. To call him that, however, is to leave off a single letter from what, more properly, should be his title. Beelzebub — so etymology informs us — was the god of little things. He was the Lord of Flies. That is what the word literally means. And it has remained for modern science to disclose the dangers of the common house-fly.

Moreover, in the regulation of our daily lives — as all of us know to our chagrin — the things that most often get upon our nerves and exasperate us into loss of self-control are the biting, teasing, buzzing little cares and troubles that seem continually to be coming back and having to be brushed away. " Who has not observed," says a writer, "how wonderfully the mere insect cares which are ever on the wing in the noonday heat of life, have power to sting and to annoy even giant minds around which they sport, and to provoke them into most unseemly war? The finest sense, the profoundest knowledge, the most unquestionable taste, often prove an unequal match for insignificant irritations; and a man whose philosophy subdues nature, and whose force of thought and purpose gives him ascendancy over men, may possess in his own temper an unvanquished enemy at home."

" We rise to meet a heavy blow;
Our souls a sudden bravery fills;
But we endure not always so
The drop by drop of little ills.

81

A Confusion of Tongues

"The heart which boldly faces death
Upon the battle-field, and dares
Cannon and bayonet, faints beneath
The needle points of frets and cares."

There is a kind of compensation, however, in the fact that what is true of the things that irritate and sting us, is just as true of the things that contribute to our pleasure and promote our happiness. Much of the joy and cheer and buoyant optimism of this world is due to very trivial and unimportant happenings and causes. Many of the happiest and most contented persons whom we know are they who can take the ordinary occurrences of daily life and find in them deep fountains of perpetual joy and satisfaction. It is the laughter and the love of little children, the hand-grasp of a friend, the word or act of affection or regard, the burst of sunlight on a radiant morning after the storm has passed — it is things like these that go to make up the great sum of human hope and cheer. " Pound St. Paul's Cathedral into atoms," said wise old Dr. Johnson in the hearing of the assiduous Boswell, " and consider any single atom, and it is, to be sure, good for nothing : but put those atoms together and you have St. Paul's Cathedral. Even so," continued the Sage, " it is with human felicity, which is made up of many ingredients, each of which may be shown to be very insignificant."

" Oh, the little more, and how much it is :
And the little less, and what worlds away."

Little things indeed ! When accurate measurements are made, and the whole to which each stands related is considered, we learn that there are no little things. It is out of the little book of some simple, unconsidered word or act that we often read with accuracy, and with more or less completeness, the truth of a person's entire character. The fragment is a portion of the whole and the part informs us of the thing from which it came to be detached. The other day some shells fell suddenly and burst, doing not a little damage, in the quiet streets of Dunkirk, on the English Channel. The townsfolk were taken utterly by surprise. Whence came the shells? The enemy was miles away. Some surmised that a submarine might have fired them. Others said that an aeroplane must have dropped them. But this was all guesswork. No one had explained the mystery. At length, however, some little pieces of the shell were found and taken to a man of science. He examined them, carefully measuring the metal and the arc of the shattered bits that had been put into his hands. And from his calculations it was learned that the shells must have been enormous, coming from a gun of huge caliber and at range of more than twenty miles.

In similar fashion, people often tell us what they are by their little, unconsidered acts of kindness or of love. The deeds which they think of least, and often never meditate at all, constitute a very safe criterion for the measurement of their goodness.

In our American calendar of heroes and martyrs, we call to mind, each year, the superlative services of Lincoln first, and then of Washington. With reverence we renew in ourselves the undying recognition of their great and high examples, their characters and lives. What is it, however, that we love to linger on longest, and never tire of having reiterated to us in sermon, memoir, or address? It is not, I think, the great moments in those wonderful careers. It is not the silent, solemn men preparing proclamations, or face to face with mighty problems in the nation's destiny and life. These are the great moments as commonly conceived and, of course, these things can never be forgotten. They constitute history and have been written for all time. But the things we never tire of, the things we treasure in significant detail, are the simple, homely, human acts which, in their own time, brought these men so near the hearts of their countrymen, and which make of their memories vital, stirring motives in our lives to-day. This is more particularly true, perhaps, of the great Lincoln with his deep and tender

nature. We see him comforting the heart
of the mother who came to ask the par-
don of her son, or sitting in the hospital
at the bedside of some wounded boy.
We hear him saying: " Do not ask me
to approve these executions. There are
too many widows already in this land."
We recall his half-humorous remark
when it was urged upon him that all
deserters be shot: " I do not see how
shooting would make them any better."
These are the " perfect tributes " to the
goodness of a great man and the greatness of a good man : only little things,
but how significant.

There are many persons who are ca-
pable of great acts, and who pine for
opportunities to do them, but who forget
about the ordinary ways of showing heroism and displaying the capacities they have
for generosity, self-sacrifice, and helpful-

ness. When this War is over and we return to the normal and the peaceful, great as the relief will be, the reaction also will be great. We shall come back from reading about and hearing about innumerable deeds of conspicuous bravery and service, not to speak of patient suffering and endurance under conditions beyond our powers to conceive — we shall come back from these to the ordinary burdens, cares, and perplexities of daily life. And when this happens — thrice blessed as the time will be — it is bound to make the world appear, at first, uninteresting, flat, and tame. The one redeeming feature of this present crucifixion is the quiet, steadfast way in which great deeds are done, great risks encountered, and great suffering borne. It brings to us all a deeper and a truer understanding of the strength there is in human nature, and of the extent of unused human energies. We have come to think it wholly natural that our boys should cross the ocean to drive French ambulances or to volunteer for service in the trenches: that women should enlist as nurses, whether to tend the wounded or to fight the foe of typhus. All this is tingling in the air and, consciously or unconsciously, affecting our entire estimate of values. But it cannot last forever. A return will come in time to the quiet ways of peace.

The present, therefore, is a good time in which to reflect upon the fact that the everyday routine of life supplies us all with abundant opportunities for bravery and heroism, not to speak of ways and means for showing courage, offering help, and doing deeds of real devotion. The truest heroes, the most useful fighters, and the most faithful workers are often to be found in the very homes that adjoin our own and on the streets that day by day we walk. Here are women who make the best of burdens, cares, and losses, smiling through tears that blind. Here are men of grim and iron resolution, who keep their failures and their sorrows to themselves, determined that their own crosses shall not bear upon the shoulders of any other. Here are men and women who give the world the best they have each day, in the trenches of stern duty and along the lines of earnest, faithful, honest, and effective service. What the world most needs, and will soon be crying out for once again, cannot be classed as signal acts, nor stirring deeds, nor memorable lives; but just simple, ordinary acts and deeds and lives of goodness, honor, justice, purity, and patience. It is these that will make our households purer, our cities cleaner, our civilization higher, more just, and more fraternal. Though the people living lives like these and doing deeds of only simple justice and integrity, "be not sought for in the council of the people," as the old Apocryphal writer puts it, "nor be exalted in the assembly; though they sit not on the seat of the judge, nor understand the covenant of judgment; . . . yet, without these, shall not a city be inhabited, nor shall men sojourn, or walk up and down therein. For these maintain the fabric of the world, and in the handiwork of their craft is their prayer."

And if, for a moment, we enter a higher sphere, we shall find that what has been said — together with much that cannot well be uttered — applies

with no less force to the teachings and
the inspirations of that phase of human
experience which we know and speak of
as Religion. We know — all of us know
— the impressions of awe and reverence
and wonder that are made upon us by
the sublime, the stupendous, and the in-
frequent in nature. We bend the knee
when we come face to face with the unfamiliar and the far. Our hearts " leap
up " when we " behold a rainbow in the
sky." But we also know — or at least
we ought to know — that the same deep
feelings and the same high impulses may
be kindled by the presence of the familiar and the near, if we but see and understand these as they are.

The gifted author of *A Window in
Thrums*, looking at the world from a
little cottage in the Highlands of Scot-
land, once said of a boisterous brother

author who had roamed and written round the world, that he had yet to learn that "a man may come to know more of life, staying at home by his mother's knee, than by swaggering in bad company over three continents." And we may surely say the same in regard to the fountains of our higher inspiration and the knowledge that pertains to things of spiritual value. The little and the near have all the glory and the romance of the great and the distant, if we have but hearts to understand and wisdom to perceive.

> "We lack but open eye and ear
> To find the Orient's marvels here ;
> The still, small voice in autumn's hush,
> Yon maple wood the burning bush."

The greatest and most marvelous things in life are ever nearest to us. It is the deadening influence of custom that causes us to think that what is familiar is also commonplace. "Breath in our nostrils, light in our eyes, flowers at our feet," generous instincts in our hearts, and duties that our hands are restless till they lay firm hold upon — these, as Bishop Thorold says, are little things that loom up large when we have found a correct perspective.

Could we pass but a single day with the Master, or with one who had the Master's spirit, the little world of every-day events around us would take on suddenly a high and sacred meaning. Stars would burn their way into our souls, and winds that blow as they list, with summer heat and winter cold, would remind us that we know not whence we have come, nor whither we shall go, but only that God's heaven arches over us. The tongue of the lisping child would tell us of a Father's love; the sparrows as they chirp and flutter in our streets would bespeak a Higher Life encircling all; and the people as they pass, whether busy in their work or careless in their play, would all be seen to be members of the same great human family. O God, how blind we are; how dull of heart and dense to understand! We move about in worlds of which we see and know not one one-hundredth part. And yet we talk of unbelief and lack of ground for faith!

Let us but learn to do the will of God in little ways; let us but build Him temples for his worship from out the common-place of everyday existence; then shall everyday existence be seen to be a miracle; then shall our separate beings find their center in a Higher Being whose law and life are manifest in all that lies about us — in what is small as well as what is large.

Chapter Five

MAKING THE BEST OF THINGS

MAKING THE BEST OF THINGS

THE Great Apostle, writing to his friends at Rome, took occasion in one connection to remark that he rejoiced in tribulation. And he gave as one reason for his exultation in it, the fact of his persuasion that "tribulation worketh patience, and patience experience, and experience hope." In re-reading the words the other day, I found myself wondering whether many persons, starting with tribulation, would have worked things out in any sequence such as that: tribulation, patience, experience, hope. Notice the order. It was progress onward from darkness into light; and from storm and flood into sunshine and calm waters.

Some of us, I fancy, — and I am not disposed in any way to underrate the bravery and cheerfulness of human nature, — some of us would have felt inclined to suggest a course the very opposite of that. Tribulation, we would have said, worketh discouragement; and discouragement means doubt, and doubt induces anxiety and apprehension. That is to say, there are many persons who have learned from life to be on their guard and not to hope too much. In the language of the day, they preach " Preparedness ": and preparedness implies the expectation of trouble.

The Great Apostle, however, was not that kind of man. Life had taught him not so much to fear as to hope; not to anticipate evil, but to look for good. The seed of sorrow might fall, indeed, into the furrows of his soul. They might take

root and grow up there; they might put
forth leaves and branches. But they would
grow up into the sunlight, and they would
blossom through the sunlight into hope.
Those words, therefore, give clear and
definite expression to the practical philosophy of a very wise and energetic individual whose life was crowded with trouble, uncertainty, and loss. Were we to
put that philosophy into the homely language of everyday life, we would say, I
suppose, that it was his studied principle
to make the best of things. It will be
worth our while, therefore, to consider
what it means to "make the best of
things": to see how tribulation may work
out patience, and patience build up an experience that blossoms into hope.

None of us are so favored in this world
as not to be acquainted with sorrows,
disappointments, failures, and anxieties.

A Confusion of Tongues

Let our lots be never so fortunate and successes never so frequent, we still are very constantly confronted with things that are not in all respects as we should like to have them. Strong though we are and resourceful as we may become, Fate is our master still; and the only wise and profitable course for us to pursue is just to make the best of whatever burdens we may be called upon to bear. And yet, how many of us do the very opposite of this and make, in no wise the best, but almost the very worst, of unfavorable circumstances and conditions. There is a marked tendency among people to answer disappointment and failure by bitter and vehement complaint, by sullen moodiness, or by retirement into a phase of selfishness that reacts most unpleasantly upon others. With some persons it is always possible to tell by the nature

of their moods when things have gone
wrong. If their latest investment has
turned out poorly, they repeat the quota-
tions of the market in the sullenness of
their demeanor. Because one little element in fortune has been against them,
their entire attitude toward life becomes
affected, and they act as if they thought
it made things better to represent them
as entirely bad.

There are, of course, persons of another type in this world. All of us know
them and rejoice to know them, while we
seek to follow in their footsteps as we can.
These are the men and women who
never let their secret sorrows cast the
slightest shadow upon their daily actions.
Failures seem only to impel them toward stronger resolution, while tribulation works with them as it worked with
the Apostle Paul. It was said, for in-

stance, of the masterful William of Orange, whom history has called "the Silent," that the thicker came to be the difficulties ahead of him, and the more threatening the plots for his assassination, the calmer and more cheerful grew his bearing. Like a rock in mid-ocean, unmoved by the waves and billows of misfortune, he embodied for his people at once the deep foundations of their national cause and the majestic strength of human nature at its best. But "the best" is something very high. The best is never the result of compromise. And I am persuaded of the fact that there are in this world many persons who simply do not understand what it means to make the best of things. Such persons seem to think, for instance, that making the best of things means no more than silent, stern endurance and an attitude of uncom-

plaining resignation. This — in a superficial sense — was the ideal that was
cherished by those noble old philosophers,
the Stoics. They schooled themselves to
rise superior to Fate. It should never
crush them, was their proud assertion.
Outwardly they might be bent and lame,
like Epictetus; but inwardly they would
be erect and calm. Though tempests
were to beat against them, they would
not complain; and though the stars in
the sky were darkened, the light within
should not be dimmed.

Sometimes we see on the bleak and
rugged seacoast of New England — at
Beverly, perhaps, or Mount Desert — a
twisted, gnarled, and stunted oak or
cedar against which the wild storms of the
stern Atlantic have beaten for years. It
clings with seasoned fiber to the cold
and sullen rock, living and growing in

spite of everything. But it has grown away from the winter winds, turning its back — as it were — to the quarter from which they blow. That is nature's symbol of the silent, sturdy, uncomplaining individual who refuses to be conquered and who *seems* to be making the best of things. There is pathos — there is grandeur, even — in the type. We cannot say, however, that it reaches the heights to which human nature *may* attain. We cannot say that it exhausts the possibilities of human achievement, leaving nothing to be desired. There is something that is higher still, and something that is more complete.

An ideal rises up before us as we contemplate this Stoic type — an ideal presenting qualities not so much in opposition as in addition to the Stoic qualities. It is the ideal we know as Christian. And

Christian teaching says: Let the storms of life, together with its sunshine and its beauty, have share in developing your capacity for growth and your strength of soul. For tribulation worketh much more than mere patience and endurance. It worketh deep and rich experience, and experience is the soil out from which grows the most tenacious hope. Does such attainment seem, perhaps, too much to expect of any human? Many of the moral torch-bearers of this world have added luster to their lives as well as illumination to our own in just this very way. Let us look at some few of the lives that illustrate the thing I mean.

Here, for instance, is the author of that hymn which has come to be so great a favorite in many churches —

"O Love that wilt not let me go,
I rest my weary soul in thee."

How many people, I wonder, know the history of the author of that hymn? It is worth knowing: it is worth remembering. The hymn was written by George Matheson: and George Matheson was a clergyman in charge of a large parish in Edinburgh. He was completely blind; yet he preached from Sunday to Sunday, conducted the service of worship which he had learned by heart, and administered his church affairs for many years. Surely he had made the best of things when, out of dark experience, he could write —

> "O Light that followed all my way,
> I yield my flickering torch to Thee.
> My heart restores its borrowed ray
> That, in thy sunshine's blaze, its day
> May brighter, fairer be."

But he, of course, is only one of many men who have pushed on and achieved, perhaps *because* a mighty struggle was

required. In the early days of the Re-
formation movement, when intellectual
and religious Europe was in a state of
turmoil and upheaval, so that it was not
safe for Martin Luther to be left at large,
his good and brave friend, the Elector of
Saxony, out of the kindness of his heart,
carried him off and shut him up in his
lonely castle on the Wartburg. The
solitude was irksome to the impetuous
Reformer. He chafed at the restraint,
holding it to be cowardly. For his own
part, he would have preferred to take
his chances in the world of men. But
the situation was one of which, at least,
he made the best. In the quiet of his
long captivity he resolutely set to work
to translate the Bible into German. And
in due course of time this Bible in the
vernacular came to be the very source
and fountain-head of a new life and lit-

109

erature for his people. Through it Martin Luther was enabled to spread the Word much more widely, indeed, than he ever could have done in liberty.

Or, take another instance that has similar features. Campanella, an Italian monk, was suspected of heresy. Persecuted and finally arrested, he was held in prison for long years. Under restraint, however, and in darkness, his restless spirit sought and found release. Denied the solace of the outer sun, he had a vision of a new and higher state of civilized existence that some day might dawn, and he wrote out, though in darkness, the treatise which he called the *City of the Sun*.

At the present time, with the change that has come in religious thought and the lessened emphasis upon personal salvation, not many of us are familiar with

Pilgrim's Progress. Few books in the
world, however, have been so widely
read. And Bunyan wrote that extraordinary volume, so full of vivid pictures,
so lifelike in its allegories, under circumstances very similar to those of which
Luther and Campanella made the best:
Pilgrim's Progress was written in the
squalid county jail at Bedford.

And thus it is in times not alone of
outward but of inward captivity and pain
and loss. The duty rests upon us all, not
simply to endure uncomplainingly the
various vicissitudes of our lives, but to
see to it that they develop in us greater
kindness, sympathy, courage, and consideration. Dante, surely, made the best
of exile from his beloved Florence when
he worked out, in his "wander years,"
the wonders of the *Divine Comedy;* and
Tennyson did the same, when, out of

the jarring notes of a youthful sorrow, he made the melodies of *In Memoriam.* And in countless instances, and in wider ways, this law of growth has been exemplified. Let us for a moment, therefore, look at matters from a larger point of view. When individual men and women seem to disappoint us, we may often find comfort and encouragement in turning to mankind. It was Plato who said long ago that his interest was not so much in men as in man.

In spite of the many failings and manifest shortcomings of the human individual, it can be said with the most literal truth that the human race has nobly, and even grandly, made the best of things. For instance: let us suppose that as human creatures we had accepted complacently and philosophically all our inherent limitations and restrictions. Where would be the glory and the grandeur of human progress? Suppose that the members of the human species had said to themselves: "No: we have not the keen glance of the eagle, nor the swift foot of the antelope, nor the great strength of the mastodon, nor the sharp sense of many a wild creature of forest and field. It is most unfortunate that such is true. But let us not complain; let us rather accept things as they are." Suppose that that had been a characteristically human attitude of mind. Where would have been the telescope and the microscope? And where our swift-rushing servants of steam and electricity? Because that was *not* man's mental attitude; because in a large sense — which also was a literal sense — men made the best of the shortness of their sight, and the slowness of their feet, and the dullness of their outward senses,

we to-day are looking off into measure-
less miles of space, and outspeeding far,
with our various contrivances, the swift-
est-footed of God's creatures. Making
the best of things like these has meant
miracles of wonderful invention; it has
meant a tremendous addition to the powers, capacities, and possibilities of human
attainment; and by just so much it has
increased the endowment of every child
born into the world.

The history of a period less remote
and of a sphere of activity more familiar
contains still further revelation of our
present-day indebtedness to those who
have wrestled with hard things that
they might find therein some blessing.
A generation since there was great confusion and distress among students of religion. Religious thought was passing
through one of the stormy periods of its

growth. Those marvelous discoveries of
science with which we are all perfectly
familiar to-day were then first divulged;
and they were very clearly in antago-
nism with many of the cherished teachings
of religion. The two seemed to be incom-
patible. The Bible, it was said, could not
be true were evolution also true. There
came to be a struggle, therefore, of
great intellects; and this struggle was
painfully repeated in many an individual
heart and conscience. Many persons
who thought themselves informed, and
who wished above all things to be honest, gave up the cause of faith. They
said, "We do not know. It is all a
mystery." And they called themselves
henceforth the *Not-knowers*, or *Agnostics*. From their point of view, only the
cold and cheerless tenets of skepticism
and materialism seemed to be consistent

with intellectual integrity; and they prophesied that all the world must come in
time to occupy their position. They made,
as they thought, the best of things. As
it has proved, however, it was not these
Stoic agnostics but another group of
thinkers, fully as sincere and with somewhat wider outlook, who really made the
best of these discoveries.

These were the thinkers who argued:
"This seems to be the truth. But, if it
be truth, it is of God. Therefore, there
must be inspiration in it: there must be
ground for hope and faith and joy." Ar-
guing thus, these scholars accepted the
unwelcome offerings of science; with
patience they dwelt upon the cold, for-
bidding theories of evolution, universal
law, and all the rest; and lo, these stones
of science were found to contain the very
bread of life. Through them was re-

vealed a new vision of the purposes and providences of God; and in the light of this clearer, higher vision, the little old beliefs of the Fall of Man, and one inspired Book, and special miracles done long centuries ago, have been worked over into the Ascent of Man, and the Bible of the human race, and the endless miracle of day and night, seed-time and harvest, birth and death and endless resurrection. Tribulation worked out patience, and patience has widened into deep experience and hope. It was thus that religion came to make the best of science.

And now, behold, another period of even greater trial and confusion has come upon religion and the churches of the Christian faith. It has been brought about by war. And war, so awful always in itself, has been made more awful than it ever was before by the way in which the inventions and appliances of science have been prostituted to its causes. It is indescribably terrible: the whole world suffers tribulation. Doubts rise up and lay hold upon us all — doubts in regard to God and man and human life in the future. For my own part, however, I cannot help believing that if we are only patient and wait until the world has worked out a great body of deep experience, then, in this case as in all the others, experience will furnish the sure foundations for new hope and joy. There is nothing much more trying than uncertainty. When what we think the Right is worsted, we are hard beset by doubts. But when men stand up — as they do — stronger, purer, braver for their struggles; when, through struggle, it is seen that vision becomes clarified, then our faith returns. And it returns stronger than it ever has been before. And so I doubt not that the best will be made, in time, of the experiences that the world is passing through just now. When, because of them, Peace becomes more highly valued; when the nations face more resolutely toward the light; when, in a word, the human race becomes more human, then shall we be able to read the meaning of this distressing epoch in the history of the world — and to read it to our moral and spiritual gain.

Then let us lay a solemn tribute down at the feet of all those who have gone forward with courage, through the gates of tribulation into pastures green with hope and rich in great productive power. As they went they were strengthened, helped, encouraged from on high. For this is ever true in life: that helping we are helped, and struggling we are given strength, and looking up we are lifted up until we come to feel ourselves a part of something larger, higher than ourselves. Thus, when we put forth effort to make the best of things — of sad things and of hard things — we find ourselves made strong to bear things that are sad and hard. Our faith becomes deep-rooted and is strengthened in the process; while, in seeking for the good, we come to a larger and a truer knowledge of the ways and laws of God.

> " For life is good, whose tidal flow
>   The motions of God's will obeys :
>   And death is good, that makes us know
>   The Life divine which all things sway.

> " And good it is to bear the Cross
>   And so the perfect peace to win ;
>   And naught is ill, nor brings us loss,
>   That brings the light of heaven in."

Chapter Six

HOW TO CHOOSE

HOW TO CHOOSE

I wish to begin what I have to say on the subject of *How to Choose,* by holding up for contemplation two familiar pictures. They are very old pictures, but both of them have a modern meaning. Each of us can put them in the frames of personal experience and hang them on the walls of our individual lives.

The first picture is thoroughly Oriental. Two men, in flowing Eastern dress, are standing on a spur of rising ground. We see their figures clearly silhouetted against a background of bright blue sky. They are Lot and Abraham: and Lot is making his choice. The two men are kinsmen. Up to this time they

123

have lived together on the best of terms. But their servants have begun to quarrel, and the two have come to feel that they must part. It were better for them to separate as friends, and not to wait until they have become involved in the disagreements of their followers.

Abraham is the older of the two. And out of his large and generous nature he has said to his friend and kinsman: "You choose, my brother. The whole land is here before us. There is room enough for both. If you will take the right hand, then I will go to the left: or, if you prefer the left hand, I will travel to the right."

So the younger man, full of rejoicing, probably, that the choice is his, goes up on a ridge of rising ground and throws an eager glance around. On the one side he sees the shadowy outlines of distant mountains, the jagged peaks of which are sharp against the sky. It is evident that the land in that direction is a land of great uncertainties — a wild and rugged land where toil and enterprise will be required. In the other direction, however, it is different. He sees there a sunlit plain that is watered by a winding river. It is an open, fertile, pleasant land. Indeed, it seems a very garden of the Lord, with its clustering vines and hanging fruit. It is a land for indolence and ease, with no tangled valleys to explore and no rocky hills to plough and plant with care and difficulty. And so with careless joy Lot chooses it. Calling his servants together he journeys east, into the land of Jordan. And lo, you remember the result. His choice involved his ruin. He sank into the luxurious and sinful ease of Sodom and Gomorrah, which the Lord at last destroyed because of their iniquity.

That is a picture from the realm of legend. Side by side with it let me hang a companion-piece which is, perhaps, more familiar and which was painted by mythology. A youthful shepherd, by the name of Paris, is feeding his flocks on the sloping hillsides of Mount Ida. In the sunlit morning of his life his days seem full of promise. And now, descending from Olympus, three heavenly beings come with word from Zeus that he — Paris — must decide a dispute which exists among them. A controversy has arisen as to which of them is most beautiful. And the father of gods and men has sent them to the unsophisticated youth that judgment may be rendered. The three present their claims, seeking to influence the decision by their various promises of reward. One of them says that, if he will decide in her favor, she will give him power and great riches. The second says that she will endow him with great glory and wisdom among men. And the third agrees that he shall have the most beautiful woman in all the world to be his wife. The youth must choose. It is so decreed.

And he chooses. Putting aside power, putting aside wisdom, he yields to the allurement of the senses. And the choice, according to the old mythology, not only involved at last his own ruin, but brought upon the world the tragedies and losses of the Trojan War.

These two pictures are suggestive because of the fact that they are so intensely and supremely human. We can all of us see ourselves in the center of each canvas. The positions of Lot and Paris are how often our own positions, and their perplexity our perplexity. Like them we have to choose. Again and again, year after year, week after week, day after day, hour by hour we have to make our choices. Which way shall we go? Which prospect and which promise seems the best? Sometimes the choices are only trivial—or at least appear so. And then again, with sinking sense of dread, we perceive that a long and important series of events will inevitably follow from the thing we choose. In moments such as these we often wish some Zeus or Abraham were at hand that we might say to him: "I do not want this privilege you give me. I would rather let the choice be yours. Choose for me and I will abide by your decree."

The choices of life: how numerous they are, how difficult and troublesome.

How easy and how simple life would be
without them; how free from anxiety,
from deep despondency, and the after
sense of mistaken judgment. And yet
— how uninteresting also. There is an
old and somewhat unfamiliar proverb
which says, "He who has a choice is
tortured." We often long to run away
from the great decisions of life; to post-
pone them; to get some one else to assume them for us and so ourselves escape
the torture. None the less, we all know
full well that the power and privilege to
choose is one of the greatest dignities
with which God in his wisdom has endowed us. It belongs to all that is wor-
thiest in duty and in destiny. Every
temptation in life implies a choice. Shall
we yield ourselves, the question is, to be
led away by some lower impulse, or
shall we swear renewed allegiance to

life's higher motives? The use of every leisure hour implies a choice. The books we read; the companionships we form; the activities in which we engage; the very thoughts we think and the pleasures we pursue — all these and how many other things are largely matters left to our choice. The Abraham of a higher unseen Power stands beside us and we hear the words: " The whole land is before you; you may take the mountains on the right hand or the meadows on the left. Choose, therefore; the privilege is yours."

Now whoso chooses well, lives well: since life is the sum of innumerable choices. For my own part, therefore, the longer I live and the more I see of people, the higher I incline to value the somewhat prosaic quality of good judgment. It does not seem to me that I underestimate in any way the significance of brilliancy or talent of high order. All of us know how much these may accomplish and for how much they should count. Moreover, I am very certain that I do not forget the importance of industry and perseverance. Innumerable are the cases in which the plodders and hard workers of the world have outstripped and left far behind the gifted and the highly endowed who lacked the capacity for continuous effort and application. Neither do I minimize the value of right instincts, pure motives, high desires, and noble impulses. These form the groundwork of all conduct: they are the qualities that make up good behavior. What I have in mind, however, and feel distinctly sure about, is this: without good judgment all these other things may be miserably wasted. Sympathy is beautiful; but it sometimes goes astray. Right impulses are noble; directed right, they are still more noble. People frequently are good, without being good for very much. We all admire perseverance; but we admire it most when we see it well applied, along lines that are likely to prove productive. As for brilliancy, great capacity, exceptional gifts of one kind or another — how constantly they seem to count for almost nothing save moral ruin and disaster.

One of the saddest things in life is the waste of life. Bright promises fade away; careers, beginning well, take some unfortunate turn, make some mistaken choice, and close in disappointment. Good judgment, therefore, — which is the capacity for choosing well and making wise decisions, — constitutes what we may call the rudder of the ship of life. It contributes not to the speed but to the safety of the voyage. It is the thing that guides us toward a goal, that keeps us on our course, and that helps us to avoid the reefs and shoals and dangerous headlands which form a part of every voyage. As compared with the throbbing engine, or the spreading sails, it may seem of little moment or interest. But without it, both sails and engine would lead life to disaster. Let us take some thought, then, of the choices of life. Let us consider how we may avoid the fate of Lot and escape the error that brought disaster upon Paris.

And first of all, we shall do wisely to recognize the fact that people are largely known by their choices. What we choose, in other words, is a pretty accurate index of what we are. We know the character of Lot, for instance, by that single choice of his. We know that he was selfish,

133

since he did not hesitate to take what seemed to be the best of all the land; and we know that he was indolent, for the reason that he chose the locality that promised least of effort and hard work. In just such fashion all of us give almost certain proof, each day, of what we are by what we choose.

"If God should stand before me, and hold out to me in his right hand Truth, and in his left hand the ever-restless search for Truth; and should say to me, 'Choose: you may have whichever you prefer'; I would bow reverently to his left hand, which held the search for Truth, and say, 'Father, give: pure Truth is for Thee alone.'" Thus spoke Lessing, the German thinker and reformer. Of course, that was only an imaginary choice. It was a picture, or a parable. And yet it tells us, without any added testimony being needed, just what the intellectual life of Lessing was and what he taught. Through its revelation we know him to have been a man who set his face against all dogmatism and who decried all claims on the part of churches, or of individuals, to have arrived at Truth.

And what shall we say of the actual choices that all of us set down in the book of life each and every day, telling just as truly as did Lessing's hypothetical choice the nature of our lives and characters. They are, many of them, trivial; but even the least of them gives clear indication of that from which it has sprung. Here, for instance, is a woman who constantly regrets, if she does not openly complain, that she has no leisure for reading. And yet, if you observe her week by week, you will notice that she squanders, either in idleness or in idle occupations, many precious hours **that,** with a little resolution, might be given to interests that count. She does not know it; the process goes on silently; but she actually does choose, after all; and she chooses the part that is unworthy.

And here, it may be, is a man who is closely related to her by the ties of moral kinship. He is absorbed in business. Were it not for business, he tells us, he would willingly do something for the public service. You perceive, however, if you give your attention to the matter, that he has time and strength for all that he really cares about. The truth with regard to this man is that he chooses, first of all, to serve himself. And his silent choice betrays his character.

What both of these people need to complain about is not the lack of time, but the lack of right habit and of resolution sufficiently strong to rearrange and redeem time. "Time," said old Benjamin Franklin, "is the stuff of life." And he might have added that it is a most elastic stuff. It stretches almost in proportion to the amount of pressure that we put upon it. The choice is ours. Time comes to us with gifts that we may either take or leave; make use of wisely or ignorantly squander. It was Emerson, you will remember, who gave such exquisite form to the thing we speak of as " the procession of the days."

" Daughters of Time, the hypocritic Days,
  Muffled and dumb like barefoot dervishes,
  And marching single in an endless file,
  Bring diadems and fagots in their hands.
  To each they offer gifts after his will,
  Bread, kingdoms, stars, and sky that holds
      them all.
  I, in my pleachèd garden, watched the
      pomp,

A Confusion of Tongues

Forgot my morning wishes, hastily
Took a few herbs and apples, and the Day
Turned and departed silent. I, too late,
Under her solemn fillet saw the scorn.''

And thus it is that the days reveal us
to ourselves and to others by reason of
the choices that we make. But in addition to this fact, it is likewise important
to remember that, more than often, what
we choose is determined directly and inevitably by what we like. This is almost
always the case in minor matters: and frequently it is true when it comes to critical
decisions. The line of personal liking is the
line of least resistance, and we naturally
follow it. It results, therefore, that to
improve our choices we must, first of all,
improve our tastes. By changing the nature of the things we like, we change
the character of the things we choose.
'' No statement of mine,'' wrote Ruskin,

" has ever been more earnestly or oftener controverted than this: that good taste is a moral quality. What we like determines what we are; and to teach taste is to teach character." It is a very practical duty, therefore, devolving upon us all, to cultivate our enjoyment of the good, the true, the holy, and the pure. If by nature we do not appreciate or value the qualities which the best judgment of the world has determined to be of worth, then we need to set ourselves to *learn* to like them. Nor is it impossible to accomplish such an end. Just as seeing and studying the best works of art gradually cause us to turn away dissatisfied with any but the best; just as hearing the best music and seeing the best drama, though at first we neither understand nor enjoy them, yet gradually make us feel the emptiness and even worthlessness of what is light and feeble; so by keeping steadily before our minds the images of the good, the noble and unselfish, we educate ourselves to turn instinctively the way they lead.

Again,—and what is more important still,—in learning how to choose we need to strengthen the habit of considering, not the immediate present, not the matter of momentary satisfaction; but, rather, what is going to be permanent, and what is going to give continuous satisfaction. God has given us all the faculty of looking forward; and he has given it to us to be used. It is never a question of to-day alone, nor even of to-morrow; our choices involve the weeks and months and, it may be, the years which silently and solemnly stretch out before us. How many a disaster comes, how many a disappointment, how many a cause for long extended suffering and remorse, because we look alone at what is just before. The momentary appetite that we would satisfy; the present pleasure that we seek to gain; these rise up and obscure the things that lie beyond.

In the familiar legend Esau sold his birthright, the privilege of a lifetime, for just a dish of pottage with which to satisfy a temporary craving; and fact makes even more familiar than does the legend this tendency of our natures to choose with reference only to the passing moment. More than once we have, each of us, been guilty of Esau's mistaken choice. In all the choices that we are called upon to make, therefore, the element of time ought to be given first consideration. The Lot within us, looking down upon some pleasant, tempting valley, needs ever to be reminded of the cities of Sodom and

Gomorrah which lie beyond the range of vision, but which to-morrow, if we go that way, will claim us for their residents. Indeed, some one has said that the most important element in the moral life is the power to visualize or to feel the sensations of "the moment after." There is many a temptation, many an alluring prospect which presents itself at night, but which loses all charm when the morning light breaks around us; and there is many a desire which goads us through the day only to recede in the calm, reflective hours of night.

There is another thought, however,—a thought more important than any of those we have thus far considered, and of greater guiding worth. It is the thought, moreover, that forms the background of the two familiar pictures I hung before you at the outset and sought to have

you consider. Lot chose the Jordan valley and turned his steps in that direction
because that way appeared to promise
ease. He would find a minimum of
labor there: self-support would not be
hard. And just on that account it was
that trouble waited for him, and disaster
rose up to waylay and, finally, to defeat
him. Because there was no challenge for
his soul, his soul was ultimately lost.

In this matter of the conduct of life,
of right behavior, there is nothing that we
need to guard against much more than
just this tendency to neglect such challenge. We are much inclined in the present day to make things easy and to have
things pleasant. We begin with education. We would have our children taught
by engaging them in play. And we end
in morals and religion by avoiding what
is irksome, dark, and difficult. We have

behind us an ancestry that points a better way. But we look back at the sternness of the Puritan ideal and we hold it up, in frequent instances, to ridicule and scorn. Those grim old forefathers, we declare, imagined that if a thing was pleasant it must, therefore, be wrong; whereas whatever was hard and disagreeable they considered to be right. They chose the way that was difficult and they set themselves to do and to endure. And I believe that in doing so they chose the better part. It seems to me, when I look back at the lives those Puritans lived, and the work they did, and the characters they shaped —it seems to me that we might find in their ideal a thing not to laugh at half so much as to live by. Whenever two ways lie before us, one of which is easy and the other hard, one of which requires no exertion while the other calls for resolution

and endurance, — happy is the man and
blessed the woman who chooses out the
mountain path and scorns the thought of
resting in the valley. These are the men
and women who are destined, in the end,
to conquer and succeed.

When in doubt, select the harder path,
the steeper way, the sterner claim. Does
that appear too rigorous a rule to lay
down for the conduct of our daily lives?
At least we all know this : that the way
of service is the way of self-denial. God
means this life of ours to be a battle, not
a holiday excursion. He has made our
natures such that only as we overcome
do we grow. Our happiness results not
from receiving but from reaching. I look
back to the teachings which we seek to
make the guide and inspiration of our
lives and this I find is what the Master
taught. His way was a way of struggle,

not of ease; of sacrifice and not enjoyment. He called to men and bade them lift the cross. I look around me at the way this world is ordered and I find the same great law at work. It is they who choose or who find themselves compelled to take the mountain-path; who spurn the valley with its languorous ease; who fit themselves for service; who lift the cross, — it is they who find the prizes that life has in keeping for the brave.

Yes, and what is more: I look at men and women such as those we live with, work with, talk with day by day; and I realize that always in their higher, truer moments, always when the cause is great and the call defined, they follow this same guiding principle. Without doubt, the descendants of Lot are many — they who love the easy path which lies along the Jordan valley: but the descendants of

How to Choose

Abraham are as the multitude of the stars in the heavens, and they shine as brightly.

When my faith burns dim, therefore, and the moments of depression come, I turn for strength to think of the hard things and the brave things and the great things which human beings calmly choose to do. I turn to the men and women who, in times like these, make such choice. I see them in an endless row, radiant, joyous, patient, as they go out to serve at posts of danger. Undaunted and serene, they approach the gates of death and pass them without fear.

Yes: it is the glory of the human being that he does not fear to choose the arduous. For

"There is no life except in death,
There is no gain except by loss;
No glory but by bearing shame,
No triumph save beneath the Cross."

Chapter Seven

THE "IF" AND "THOUGH" OF FAITH

THE "IF" AND "THOUGH" OF FAITH [1]

JACOB is one of the most contradictory characters in the Bible. One never knows exactly where to find him. A double-minded man, he was certainly unstable in all his ways. He was devout, but he was likewise deceitful. He looked above for mercy, but he looked around for ways of self-advancement. He was good at setting up altars, but he was equally good at setting up a trade. He was ready in making religious vows, but he was no less ready in making business deals. He was not averse to taking advantage of heavenly

[1] George Hodges, *Christianity between Sundays,* p. 200.

assistance, but neither was he averse to taking advantage of his family and friends. As he appears on the pages of the Bible, he was a sharp and calculating hand at driving a bargain. When he saw his brother faint with hunger, he offered him a mess of pottage in exchange for the birthright — a precious possession in those times, a thing for a lifetime. And he got it. He secured it, however, by deceit and he lived to be punished for his sin. Like many an inveterate trader, too, he sometimes was outwitted. We remember, for instance, the compact he made with his uncle Laban. He agreed to serve his uncle for seven years; and in return he was to receive Rachel for wife. But Laban had the family instinct and was equally unscrupulous. Instead of Rachel, at the end of seven years he gave Jacob his older daughter, Leah. And

Jacob had to make another bargain and serve another seven years.

Now this deep-grained instinct of his for making bargains he carried over into his religion. He had a vision in which God appeared to him. He was deeply impressed and he declared that he believed. But even now he was not disposed to give unless he got something in return. He built an altar and he made a vow. But his vow was accompanied by a condition. "*If*," he said, — "*if* God will be with me, and will keep and care for me; *if* God will give me bread to eat and raiment to put on, so that I come again to my father's house in peace; then shall the Lord be my God, and I will believe in him, and will worship him devoutly." His faith, as is clearly seen, had a considerable condition attached to it; his religion was accompanied by a

very big *if*. *If* I get what I want, I will
believe. *If* I am prosperous and the world
goes well with me, then will my heart
be lifted up in trust and confidence. But
otherwise let not God suppose that I can
be counted upon for reverence and worship.

In this respect, as well as in many
other ways, Jacob was the father of a
mighty race and has had a host of direct
descendants. Indeed, a great deal of religion, from the very first, has been *conditional* religion. It has been based upon
a bargain. It has rested upon an *if*. Take
the element of sacrifice, for example.
Almost all religions, in their early days
at least, have had some rites or forms
of sacrifice connected with them. Under
such influence, people have been encouraged to give up something — and often
something that was very precious. They

have taken animals, they have even taken children, and laid them bleeding upon the altar as offerings to God. And for what reason have they done it? They have done it on the basis of a bargain. They have believed that if they gave something they would receive something in return. And the more precious the thing they gave the more certain were they to receive some substantial benefit by way of compensation. Divine favor, as they saw it, could be bought. That is one side of the matter. And at times it has been a very superstitious and even sordid side.

But there is another side. It is true that faith and worship are frequently dependent upon favorable circumstance. There are many modern illustrations of the fact. We believe: but some of us believe only under certain conditions — which are generally conditions of prosperity. There are in this world, however, men and women of another fiber; whose moral and religious life has very different foundation. The basis of their faith is the subject under discussion in one of the most beautiful — and perhaps the most remarkable — of all the books of the Bible. Theirs is the deep problem and theirs the solution that lies at the heart of the drama in the Book of Job. In the Book of Job, you will remember, Satan was one of the leading characters. And Satan claimed that Job's religion was religion with an *if*. Moreover, he set about to prove that this was so.

The opening scene of the drama is laid in the heavenly regions, and upon a day when the angels had come to present themselves to the Most High. Among the others Satan, the accuser of men, appeared. He brought many charges against the sordidness and sinfulness of human beings. But God refuted him by calling attention to his servant Job, a man absolutely blameless in his piety and virtue. Satan, however, was very far from being convinced. "That's all very well," he argued, "but does Job serve God for naught? You have hedged him in and prospered him. But just take away his possessions and see what will happen." So suffering was sent to Job. His cattle were killed; his children died; his house was destroyed by a whirlwind; and Job was heart-broken. He tore his clothes; he shaved his head. "Naked," he cried, "was I born, and naked shall I return." But immediately he added, very humbly, "The Lord gave, and the Lord hath taken away. Blessed be the Name of the Lord." And in all this Job sinned not.

But Satan still was unconvinced. Some-

where there must be an *if*. "Very good,"
he said, "but possessions, after all, are
only one thing. Now touch his person."
So a loathsome disease was sent upon
Job and his misery was complete. His
wife reproached him: his friends ac-
cused him. But Job was adamant. His
soul stood firm. "Shall we receive good
at the hands of God and not evil also?
Though He slay me, yet will I trust
Him." Such was his firm and final dec-
laration. There was no *if* in Job's religion.

Here, then, are two very diverse con-
ceptions of religion. In the one case is a
religion based upon a bargain; in the
other is a religion independent of all
bargains.

That there is a great deal of Jacob-
religion in the world is an unhappy but
undeniable fact. Religion, for example,

has to do with happiness. Our faith should contribute to our cheerfulness and courage and contentment. How often it is true, however, that our happiness has an *if* attached to it. We would be happy *if:* — *if* we had more money; or were not obliged to work so hard; or had not known such heavy losses; or did not have so many causes for anxiety. A great many of us are cheerful only under certain conditions. We are bright when the sky is bright; we are sunny when the sky is clear, when the winter is well past and the signs of spring appear. When things go well with us they go well for the members of our families and for our friends. But when we have met with disappointment and rebuff at the hands of fortune or of fate, others are made to know it and to feel it quite as keenly as we do ourselves. Many persons are mercurial in more senses than they realize. Their generosity goes up, their cheerfulness, their amiability, their courage, and their faith go up, just in accordance with the atmospheric conditions, as it were, of their outward fortunes. Happiness for all these people is conditional. They are happy when it is easy and perfectly natural to be happy. But when the chill and wintry blasts of trouble blow, then their spirits suddenly go down—at times as low as zero. They are like Jacob in the wilderness. The god of happiness is their god, and they hold to him just as long as they are fed and clothed and permitted to go upon a prosperous way.

All of us know well, however, that the only genuine and worthy happiness and optimism is that which makes the best of things; which compels smiles through tears, and patient hopefulness in the face of sorrow, difficulty, perplexity, and disappointment. The cheerfulness that counts, the courage that we admire, the buoyancy of spirit that has value is that which holds a *though* in it; which comes hard; which is not simply a reflection from within of that which lies without. It is a virtue to be hopeful only when the clouds hang low and when the horizon all around is dark. It is valorous to wear a cheerful front only when we are not fed and clothed as we desire, and when the road of life is rough and hard and painful. All other happiness is based upon a sordid bargain. It lacks those inner, spiritual elements which are the essence of all true religion. And not until we shall have acquired a capacity for this other, inner happiness, shall we be able to enter into the experience of

the Great Apostle who could say that
he had learned, in whatever state he
found himself, therewith to be content.
"I know," he declared, "I have learned
the secret, both to be filled and to be
hungry, both to abound and to be in
want. I can do all things in Him that
strengtheneth me."

And what is true of happiness is still
more true with respect to duty which
forms so large a part of all religion.
The virtue of a great many persons has
an *if* in it. How many would be generous provided they had as much to do
with as others evidently have. How
many would assume some public burden
if they were not so absorbed and busy.
How many would never have fallen into
sin, nor have stained their souls with dis-
honesty, impurity, and vice, *if* temptations
had not been so strong or passions so riot-

ous. Becky Sharp, whom we may look upon as the prototype of a host of men as well as women, was convinced that " it would be easy — oh, so easy — to be good on five thousand pounds a year." Some have placed the figure higher and others altogether lower ; but nearly all of us share the great delusion or make some bargain with ourselves on the assumption that circumstances hold the secret of all virtue. With some persons it is temperament that has to take the blame ; with others it is heredity ; with others still it is conditions, or lack of opportunity, or this thing, or that. But with nearly all of us there somewhere is an *if*.

We have heard a great deal within recent years about a " living wage." We have been told that we cannot expect people to be virtuous or to hold their honor high when they are not paid for their labor enough to support themselves in decency. And I would not for a moment claim that there is not oftentimes some reason of the sort at the root of not a little of the moral laxity of our time. But what I would rather emphasize is this: that virtue cannot safely or securely rest on any Jacob-bargain of this kind. "If God will give me food to eat and raiment to put on, then God shall be my God." Such a vow is no less unsubstantial than the shifting desert sands upon which it first was made. Virtue is virtue, not so much when virtue pays and the bargain seems to be a good one, but when it cannot be seen that it does pay, and when it costs us something. Duty rises in the scale of value when the element of difficulty enters in and when resolution, strength, self-sacrifice, and courage are required.

Around the wretched *ifs* of life which so
beset the pathways that we travel, around
and high above them, rises just the one
word *though*. To be generous when we
have no great abundance and it is not
easy to be generous; to be patient when
our patience is severely tried; to be
strictly honest when just a little swerv-
ing from the path of absolute integrity
would seem to offer some reward; to be
loyal when our loyalty is tested; to be
lenient when we seem entirely justified
in feeling and in being hard; to be for-
giving and magnanimous when injury
and injustice have been done us; to be
kind when others have been cruel; to
be true when we have met with falsity,
and chivalrous when others have been
selfish; to live one's life along such lines
as these is to lift duty high above the
level of all elements of bargaining, and

to reveal it as a law of God who builds his altars in the hearts of men.

Happiness and duty : these are a large part of all pure and undefiled religion, and without them religion is a vain and formless thing. But beyond them lifts the peak to which religion, in its highest reaches, always must attain. Beyond them rises faith. And what shall we say of the faith that depends upon some *if?* What shall we say — ah, what need we say in times like these, when faith for nearly all of us has been so sorely tried? We would believe in God, men say, *if* it were not for the fact of war. We would have believed in God *if* the world had gone along its well-appointed path of peace; *if* progress had not been interrupted in this fashion; *if* the counsels of the wise and good had not been disregarded; *if* the nations would but arm against iniquity and not for objects of aggrandizement or world-supremacy.

And in cases where such distressing, world-wide conditions seem to lie outside consideration, the *if* of faith depends on things nearer home and much more personal. All of us have our individual sorrows, losses, trials, elements of suffering and pain; and nothing else is ever half so real. The universe, for all of us, revolves around our little selfhoods. It is that which comes near to us, affects us, and is part of our experience, that ever is most real. A great thinker spoke once of " der verdamte Ich " — the accursed I — which governs all our thinking, all our doing, all our understanding and conception of life and of the progress, ordering and meaning of the world. I was reading but the other day a singularly frank and interesting volume of autobiography. It was called the *Education* of the individual who wrote it. And the impression given was that the business of the world should have been to educate and develop just that special individual. Since that end had not been satisfactorily attained, the world had clearly been at fault. Its institutions were inadequate and called for radical correction. And so in lesser ways we nearly all of us, consciously or unconsciously, enter into a kind of Jacob-bargain with the mighty sphere of things within which we live and play our little parts. When things go our way, and when world events take place in accord with our philosophy of progress, then God is our God and we find it possible to believe.

But it is with faith precisely as it is with happiness and duty. Faith rises to its heights only when it can say with fervor, " Though He slay me, yet will I trust Him." Moreover, that is what it always has said in the past and that is what it is saying to-day. I look back at the generations and the centuries gone, and the great believers as they come to meet me are men and women who have suffered and have been acquainted with deep grief. They have a mighty *though* upon their lips, and not a feeble *if*. I see the martyrs and I see the heroes and I see the saints. I see them burdened to the earth, yet with eyes that look to heaven. I see them in a long procession going on a darkened way; but their faces are alight with the thought of God. I see them bearing all things, and yet believing all things; tried and yet forever trusting. And I find their archetype in the figure of the Christ upon the cross.

Nor is it different when I look at men and women all around me at the present time. Would I seek for faith — the faith that is strongest, deepest and most real? I do not go to those whose lots are easy and whose burdens light. I do not turn to the prosperous and pleasure-loving, to the light of heart and gay of soul. No: but I turn to those who have known the hard things or this world and who have fought against them; who have suffered and endured. I turn to those who have come through the waters of tribulation, and have washed their garments in the sea of pain.

And hence it is that out of all the sorrow that the world is living through at present I look to see a new and deeper, firmer faith evolve. It will be a faith that has seen the worst, and seen through it, and above it. It will be the faith of

The "If" and "Though" of Faith

the Crucified, who was lifted through his cross to triumph, and who dying prayed, " Father, not my will but Thine be done."

Chapter Eight

EXTRA PENNIES

EXTRA PENNIES

THE roads in Palestine at the present day are none too good; but they are vastly better than they were two thousand years ago. In the old days all traveling was done on foot or else on muleback. To-day the tourist goes from place to place in a comfortable carriage behind a pair of horses, and even motorcars are not unknown. If you are a stranger in Jerusalem and wish to see the sights, an agent of Thomas Cook and Son will probably persuade you to take the drive to Bethlehem. If you put yourself entirely in his hands, he will take you down in a party that goes by carriage to the Jordan, passing by the way the site of ancient Jericho. The road is not of asphalt nor has it been macadamized; but it is broad and safe, and the journey can be made in comfort.

In New Testament times, however, conditions were vastly different. The road from Jerusalem to Jericho was hardly more than a bridle-path. It ran through rough and rugged country and was so beset by brigands that it bore the name of the " bloody road." Very often travelers who went that way were attacked and robbed : sometimes they were killed. None the less, the way was frequently used by merchants, priests, and other persons of importance; for Jericho was the most thriving center eastward of Jerusalem.

It was this dangerous but familiar road which formed a background for the most famous and instructive picture that the

Master ever etched. We see, as clearly almost as though we had witnessed the entire scene, the lonely traveler who was suddenly beset by robbers who beat him, stripped him of his clothes, then fled into the hills, leaving him half dead. And now, as we look and watch there, one by one the familiar figures come along, standing out clear-cut against the far horizon. First comes into sight a Priest. He sees the wounded man and mutters portions of the Law; but he takes the far side of the road and hurries on that he may not be late for the Temple service. The next man to approach is a Levite. And he is filled with fear. He digs his heels into his mule and canters off, lest the robbers be not far away and return to catch him. And then, before the dust has settled on the road, our friend, the Good Samaritan, draws near. This is the man who, the Master said, proved himself a genuine neighbor and deserved to inherit eternal life. Let us consider for a moment just what it was he did, and let us see what his action has to teach us in the matter of the conduct of life.

As was natural enough, and simply human, he not only stopped and got off his mule and went to the wounded man, whom the Priest and Levite had passed by in fear for their precious safety; but, in addition, he administered "first aid" as it was understood and practiced in those days. He applied a mixture of oil and wine to the cuts and bruises of the injured man. And then, instead of leaving him to shift for himself, he mounted him upon his own beast and, himself walking along the narrow, hobbly way, he got him at last in safety to the nearest inn.

Nor did his care and attention end with

that. Instead of leaving him to ignorant
or indifferent attendants, he took charge
of the sufferer himself and in person saw
to it that he was lodged in comfort.
Surely now he had done the utmost that
was possible and could go, relieved in
mind, upon his way. But no. There was
one thing more — a service that crowned
the whole proceeding and lent the touch
of genuine beauty to the ministry of
mercy. The next morning, when it was
time for him to go away, he did not
simply leave a message for the man; but
he put his hand in his pocket, took out
two pence and gave them to the host,
saying, "Take care of him: and if you
spend anything more on his behalf, when
I come back I will repay you."

It was a little act, clearly in excess of
what was strictly necessary. It was an
act which many a good and generous per-

son never would have thought to do. But it made the entire ministration wonderfully and beautifully complete. This Good Samaritan did not go upon his way, joyfully making his escape from an unpleasant task with the soothing thought that he had done what was humanly necessary, and all that could be expected. Not at all. He was willing to assume new obligations, self-imposed. And that little gift in the morning light, after all that he had previously done, may be accepted as an infallible indication of the spirit of his life and the nature of his mercy. It was a thing in excess of what simple duty had prescribed; it was a gift which had the giver in it; an act of the hand which revealed the heart to be big and generous and thoughtful. And what ought those two pence—which were worth about two shillings, or a half-dollar, in the

money of the times—what ought they
to symbolize for us? What may they suggest by way of lessons that are vital, practical, and personal as we go about the
duties of our daily lives?

There are not a few among the good
people of the world, who live without re-
proach and who obey the letter of the law,
but who also live without the element of
grace and beauty in their goodness and who
lack the spirit which irradiates the outward
and the purely legal letter. All of us know
persons who are so good that we often
wonder why they cannot be a little better.
They are honest, let us say; but we wish
that they were generous also. Or they are
generous, and we wonder why they cannot be judicious. Or they are generous and
judicious, and we regret that they have
not more perseverance. Or they may
have all these things, and yet distinctly

lack those elements of cheerful willingness and happy courtesy which so illum-
ine and transform the life of duty. These
are the qualities which serve, as did the
Samaritan's two pence, to round out and
complete and beautify the whole; and we
cannot but regret the fact when they are
withheld.

We know, for instance, how it is in
matters of outward or material construction. Men are building, we will say, a
mighty arch to form some aqueduct or
bridge. They blast the quarry; they shape
the stone; they haul the great blocks to
the water's edge and lift them painfully
into place, the one upon the other. The
hard, mechanical, and dreary work goes
on, unnoticed and in silence. But now,
some unknown hand has swung the key-
stone into place and it settles down, a perfect fit, to bind the arch and give the

work completeness. And now the cheers break forth; now praise is gladly given. For the thing is finished. There is nothing lacking. The work is rounded out into a graceful and completed whole. Nor is it different with the structure that we know as life, or with the separate arches that comprise the growing and continually changing fabric we are at work upon each day. Let us look, then, with some care at these extra pennies. Let us consider how they complete and beautify a number of the acts and deeds of everyday existence.

First of all, the extra pennies symbolize the joy that should ever be the crowning element in virtue. A great many persons in this world are good without rejoicing in the laws of goodness. They give, but do not give with any gladness; they show mercy, but show it without cheerfulness. They love, but dissemble their love beneath an exterior of gruffness. They are active in business without being fervent in spirit or feeling any consciousness of serving the Lord. They weep with those who weep and sympathize with those who are sad; but they never rise to the height of rejoicing with those who rejoice —which is a distinctly harder thing. The Psalmist speaks, in a certain connection, of a man who took the statutes of the Lord and made them his *songs* throughout the days of his life. That is a thing which few persons ever do. All of us are in daily contact with men and women who find their duties a burden and who put them through as such; who accept the commandments of the Lord, but wish that conscience were not so exacting. And I am bound to say, with entire frankness, that we cannot but admire, in a way, the persistent toil in this world of those who are reluctant and unwilling. The service that comes hard, and that is done rebelliously, has something in it that is not without appeal. There is a certain element of beauty, even, in the faithful performance of the man who ploughs the field all day while having no fondness for the life of farming; and in the study of the man who holds himself to his books though all the time disliking study; and in the application of the man who attends to the detailed drudgery of business while constantly regretting that he is not able to do his part in another sphere than that of trade. All of this requires strength and calls for perseverance and resolution — qualities of a high order, indeed.

And yet, while all of us admire acts and lives like these, we know full well that there is something higher and distinctly more noble. Lives informed by such a spirit are not to be compared with those which are eager, joyous, and devoted, whether in study or toil. Unwilling service is respectability: glad and willing service is nobility and puts the doer in a higher class. "We sometimes think," it has been said, "that it is a mark of virtue to do things which we do not like: but how much greater a mark of virtue it is to like what we have to do." It is thus that stumbling-blocks are made into stepping-stones; that statutes come to be songs; and that the consciousness of duty widens to become the sense of privilege.

The difference between these attitudes of mind and spirit is like the difference we find in certain stages of a river as it makes its way and pushes onward toward the sea. There is a glory and a power none can gainsay in the early stages of the stream among the hills; gathering strength from many sources, it tumbles sheer and foaming down the lofty ledges on the mountain side, and paints the sunlight into rainbows with the tumult that it makes. For all of that, however, there is a larger power and a greater beauty in the quiet, solemn, stately river winding through the meadows it enriches, and reaching out with broadening sweep to meet the sea. The one stage has the glory of a beginning only; the other is a natural end and peaceful consummation. The one reveals the power of effort; the other shows forth the dignity of fulfillment.

And thus it is in the doing of life's duties. The end that we are nearing and should most desire is the easy and the glad performance of what is just and true and pure, of what is helpful and unself-ish. All of us are travelers; all of us are going down the familiar, well-trodden, yet forever dangerous road which leads from the Jerusalem of every birth to the Jericho which lies within the fruitful val-ley of the Jordan. Blessed, therefore, are the men and women in this world who wear no sense of effort on their brows as they go their various ways, intent on doing the little or the much of good they can, and who perform the duties of their lives with a sense of joy that has driven out all thought of sacrifice. Yes: the element of joy is as the gift of added pennies, making perfect and complete the deeds that fall to us to do as we journey down life's road.

But those added pennies symbolize another thing: they symbolize the ele-ment of unwearying patience. They were

the act of a man who was not only willing to do good but to keep on doing
good; and who, having done what he
could, went forward on his way unmind-
ful of reward. One of the tendencies that
all of us have to fight against as we journey is the tendency to become tired of
the repetition of effort we must make,
of the continuous output of energy along
lines that are forever the same, and toward ends that seem never to vary. As
life advances and the road becomes familiar, our zest departs. We get tired
of being resolute and cheerful; tired of
being merciful and generous; tired of being tolerant with other people and for-
giving of their faults; tired of helping
wounded and dejected travelers upon
life's way. The monotony of life, and its
drudgery, and the seeming fruitlessness
of effort are what oftentimes oppress

people with a dreary sense of despera-
tion almost.

There are times or seasons in life when
we are glad to do things or to bear things
which are neither easy nor considered,
for the most part, pleasant — glad to deny
ourselves in many ways and to go without what other people have in great abundance. But when the necessity for such
things continues, when the burden is not
lightened nor the load removed, then it
is that the test comes and the trial of one's
strength is made.

" Husband and wife," says a writer,[1]
" while they are young and the baby is
still a baby, play at economy as at a
game. . . . Out of books, out of good
examples, out of their own hearts they
encourage one another and quote the
whole anthology of the praise of thrift:

[1] *Confessio Medici*, pp. 121–23.

Extra Pennies

'My father was just as poor at my age as I am. My mother had to do without lots of things; besides, she had such bad health.' . . . In the profound Greek sense of the word, they have enthusiasm. Look which way they will, back, or here, or ahead, they see the sunshine. They find a sacrament in their daily bread and a miracle in the coming of the baby. To save, to wait, to scrape along, — why that is what they enjoy; that is the way to begin, the classic, heroic, historic, romantic, practical way. . . . See them, this man and this woman setting out, hand in hand, heart in heart, into an expectant world. In all life there is nothing more delightful, more inspiriting, than the sight of their bow in the clouds.

"But suppose the clouds continue, and the sky keeps gray : no storm clears the dull air and washes the streets of life :

191

only the sky is gray and the bow is gone. Slowly the sense of effort and of make-believe comes into their game of economy. They begin to long to play at something else. Once they were proud of not being rich: now the most they can compass is to be proud of not being ashamed of being poor; and sometimes even that humble pride breaks and lies in the dust."

What a picture that is of the weariness that comes so commonly over one great phase of well-doing. And I hardly need to add that this is only one of very many phases. When we look at the opposite side of the shield — at the lives of those who have leisure and abundance of privilege and opportunity — we see the same persistent tendency at work. Even privilege often palls and blessings come to look like burdens. Parents sometimes get tired of the perversities and peculiarities of their children. What they were willing to put up with and to make the best of when the children were young, they begin to fret and fume against when growth has been attained and discretion ought, they think, to have been developed. Oh, there are countless things in the lives of all of us that consume us with the sense of weariness and fretfulness and distaste. The night of discouragement sets in around us and we think that the efforts we have made and the duties we have done, have come to nothing. The world shows hardly any signs of getting better. The load of poverty is just as heavy as it ever was. Sin and vice still stalk abroad. We have put our shoulders to the work of reform; but society is just as unreformed as ever. The good Samaritans never were so numerous; but the wounded wayfarers seem to multiply as fast. Why, therefore, should we not just take our ease and let the world wag on as best it can?

When such thoughts as these oppress us, it is the lesson of the added pennies we need to learn. There are few things in this world that count for more than what the Great Apostle spoke of as " patient continuance in well-doing." It is precisely when the sky seems darkest, and the road is roughest, that added strength is called for and new endeavor is required. To toil and then to trust — to trust that the toil has not been wholly fruitless: these two are equally our duties on the journey of life. We must learn to plough and plant, and then to leave to God the matter of the increase. We must do and never doubt that, if the deed be good and honest, unselfish and sincere, it will

194

not be completely lost in the wise economy of God's great household.

And finally, those extra pennies symbolize another and a higher thing. It will be noticed that they were not given directly to the suffering brother man; instead, they were given to the keeper of the inn who was depended on to exercise protecting power. And so it is, or should be, in every instance. The final element of service which crowns and glorifies all that we have done, or tried to do, should be offered and entrusted to the Host and Keeper of the world. We are still speaking of factors that bear upon the conduct of life. And what is conduct if not the object of religion? I presume we shall agree with a famous teacher of a former generation that "conduct is three fourths of life." What then is the other fourth? The other fourth is that which lies behind and reaches through and irradiates all life. It is the consciousness of something in this world higher than we are ourselves — a Higher Will which we seek to do, a Higher Purpose which we seek to serve.

And when we have that consciousness, I cannot help believing that something very beautiful and precious is added to the ways and modes and impulses of life. It is this that takes all duty and makes of it a thing divine. It is this that adds to human mercy, helpfulness, and kindness a heavenly element and meaning. It is this that makes and keeps us kindred as we go along the narrow road that leads from darkness into light, and from time into eternity. We are not alone; it is not our personal or private wills we seek to serve. But there is a Higher Power in this world in whom we live and move and have our being; whose will we wish to serve and whose spirit gives us inspiration.

When, therefore, we have done the utmost that we can, when we have sought to know and to fulfill the highest law of human conduct, let us make one added gift and let us make it to the Host of the mighty inn wherein we lodge. Let reverence and trust and awe constitute the pence we offer — a gift of those who ask for guidance and who pray for strength.

Chapter Nine

THE DEPARTURE INTO EGYPT

THE DEPARTURE INTO EGYPT

THE Christ-Child, as a child, it will be remembered, was borne away from the place of his nativity and banished to another country. According to the legend, Herod, the king whose name is still a synonym for tyranny and cruelty and savage lust, had designs upon the infant's life. It had been prophesied that here was one who would grow up to be a mighty spiritual monarch and to overthrow the rulers of the earth. Messiah, or the Christ, according to the prophecies, would some day rule alone, having subdued all kingdoms to himself. And now — so Herod was informed — the Messiah had been born. His star had appeared in the East and wise men had arrived to do him honor.

It was in self-defense, accordingly, that Herod sought to take the child's life. And with such intent he charged the Magi to return when they had found him and reveal the place where he was laid. But Joseph, according to the story, was warned of the danger in a dream. He was told to make his way immediately into Egypt. And he did so. He arose and took the young child and his mother, by night, and departed into the distant land watered by the Nile.

How the story of that famous flight arose, we need not now consider. Neither need we take the trouble to investigate the probabilities of its accuracy. It is enough for our present purpose to recall the incident. It has been made familiar by the pictures that artists have so often painted: a man and woman, a little child between them, making their way across the broad and thirsty desert into Egypt.

Into Egypt! And what was Egypt at that time? What had it been for many centuries in the eyes of the faithful Hebrew? Why, Egypt was the land of idolatry and darkness; of luxury and license. It was the center of superstition and gross ignorance, and of mere material might and wealth. It was the land from which the older generation had escaped, thereby finding deliverance into a higher life and the moral law. Yet, into this land of darkness and of death the Christ-Child, as a child, was banished. He was borne away from the people and the land where he belonged: for his own received him and believed him not.

That history is fond of repeating itself, we all know well. We know too —

though it is not pleasant to confess it — that more than once the Christ-Child has departed into exile, being banished and his life endangered by his own. Indeed, say what we will and argue as we please, the Christian spirit, after more than nineteen hundred years, remains even to-day but a helpless little child. And now, once again banished from his own, the Child has departed into Egypt.

It is a happy and instructive thing that here in New England a certain two festivals come together every year. At the moment when the Christmas bells are just beginning to ring, and the Christmas anthems first are heard, we in New England are encouraged to take thought of our forefathers and the things for which they stood. And for two years past this conjunction of events has had in it much of profit, as it seems to me; it has been particularly well worth our while, I think, to recall the attitude of the Puritans toward Christmas. They banished all festivities and gayety. Green boughs and the lighted tree were forbidden. For, in 1644 the Long Parliament had ordered that the twenty-fifth of December should be strictly observed thereafter as a fast, and that all men should pass the day in humbly acknowledging the great sins of the nation. Since this War broke out, I confess that I have called to mind this legislation of the Puritans with a certain sort of sympathy. It has seemed to me that the Christian nations might well enough again give orders that Christmas Day should be celebrated as a fast, and that all men should be called upon to acknowledge the sins that the nations have committed in banishing from their midst the Christ-Child.

A Confusion of Tongues

A hundred years from now — yes, a thousand years from now — people will be writing about and reading about and studying still this great world-crisis of which we all, in some sense, are a part. Just as we to-day read about the decline and fall of the Roman Empire and the Mussulman invasion and the great Crusades, so, in those far-off future days, historians and philosophers and moralists will be studying this phase of social catastrophe which we are passing through. What they will say about it, no one possibly can tell. What their judgment finally will be, none of us can know.

But of this fact we can be reasonably sure: something will be said about the failure of religion. Without doubt, some reference will be made to the fact that those nations which claimed to be followers of the Prince of Peace were the ones that went to war; and that the people who had quoted approvingly the Prophet's words of a time to come when spears would be beaten into pruning-hooks and swords into ploughshares, were found to be acting under the influence of very different motives. For lo, every great discovery of science, and each wonderful invention in the arts, had been debased to the awful objects of destruction, suffering, and death.

And yet it is possible, if not to exaggerate all this, at least to misplace the emphasis and to fail to read aright the signs. In the first place, we cannot too frequently be reminded of the fact that it is not Christianity that is on trial at the present time; but men and women in their attitude toward Christianity. It is not the Christ-Child who has failed; but the unworthy followers of the Child, who have seen Him borne off into Egypt. The Christian spirit has not proved itself mistaken; the mistake lies with those who should have been—but were not—the embodiments of that spirit. The failure, if failure there has been, has been a failure of self-styled Christian people; not of the Christian faith. Here is a religion whose very essence is spirit: and men have made of it a body of doctrines. It was meant to be a point of view: and the Church has distorted it into a set of views. It is a way of living: and it has come to be interpreted as a way of looking upon life. What we need to realize, therefore, at the present time, is distinctly this: there has been something radically wrong, not with Christianity, but with our way of interpreting Christianity.

We have seemed to think that we could have a Christian civilization with-

out the Christian spirit at the heart of it
as the guiding and controlling power.
We have imagined that science and art
and education and commerce were the
forces out of which real progress could
evolve. Power, we have thought, must
be power for good, and wealth appeared
a blessing in itself. And now the nations
of the older world have seen the hollow-
ness of what they called their civilization.
They have seen that selfishness was the
thing which they had built upon, and
that their Christianity was a matter only
of the surface things of life. If, therefore, the new age is to be an improvement upon the old, there must be a new
beginning, and a beginning from the
bottom. If the form is to be different,
then the spirit that controls the form
must be different. If genuine progress
is to come, that kind of life must be

secured which alone can guarantee the progress.

It is, I take it, one of the advantages of great catastrophes and crises that they teach us where we are and what is wrong. They open our eyes to solemn facts and help us to realize wherein we have taken a false course. In this way a new beginning becomes possible and a different line of advance may be entered upon. For some years past we have been accustomed to emphasize, at the Christmas season, the great conviction that the world is steadily growing better. We have seen signs, and have pointed to them, indicative of an increasing humanity and fellowship and friendship among the peoples of all nations. Two years ago, three years ago, — in fact for generations past, — we should all have been agreed that "in the nineteen centuries

which have elapsed since the star of
Bethlehem shone above the manger of
the Prince of Peace, there has been a
steady approach toward the ideals which
the Christian religion brought to humanity." The world, we knew, had fallen
pitiably short of attainment; but at least
it was now approaching the goal. The
growth, to be sure, had been slow and
painful; but at least some measure of
growth was actually taking place. The
Child, we said year after year, the Child
of the Christmas promise was "increasing in wisdom and stature, and in favor
with God and man."

But now, it seems, we cannot say that
sort of thing. The Child has been taken
into Egypt. Men have shown themselves
quite as cruel as they were in the time
of Herod; nations have proved themselves quite as warlike; and civilization

seems no more than a veneer. We all
have been the victims of a great delusion; for now the hands on the clock of
human advancement have been set back
and, instead of pointing nearer and nearer
to the high noon of achievement, they
present such an aspect as convinces us
that the kingdom of heaven never was
so far away.

In this respect, however, it is probable
that we are grievously, although very
naturally, mistaken. It may be — I myself should not be surprised if it were
true — that not for many a year has there
been such good reason as there is just now
for putting confidence in human progress and achievement. Recently, alas,
improvement has not come; but it is no
less certain that, in countless periods in
the past, improvement *has* taken place.
And it is probable that, even now, we

are on the very eve of a marvelous new birth. Humanity is still unredeemed; but there is good reason to believe that when this War is over — this War which the great mass of the people had no hand in bringing about, and would have stopped, could they have done so — we shall find the people of the world a chastened, purified, exalted and more religious people. They will have learned their lesson — an awful lesson, to be sure; but still, they will have learned it and they will be the better for it.

Do you remember how the early Christians in Imperial Rome were forced to celebrate their Christmas? Hated and persecuted, their only places of safety and of refuge were underneath the ground, far out of sight. In the catacombs, beneath the pagan tombs on the Appian Way, places which tourists visit

213

now with weird and idle wonder, they met to celebrate the birth of Christ. In those dismal regions, where smoking torches only in part lighted up the fetid darkness, they told again the wondrous story. And one old man among them, so we read, an old man who had been hunted by the Romans and condemned to death, was bold enough to proclaim, there in the darkness, the glorious future of the Christian faith. "This roof," he said, his countenance gleaming as he pointed to the damp and solid earth above him, — "this roof hides the stars; but they are shining still. And so shall the light of our religion glow among the hosts of the righteous who are to appear through all the ages. The star of Bethlehem will never set."

It appears to me that we to-day are in a position somewhat similar to that of the early Christians, and that their word of prophecy is the very word that many of us need to take to heart at this darkened season. Especially is this word helpful for those of us who have steered our course by the stars of human progress. Those stars cannot be seen at the present moment. But they have not set. They are, believe me, just above our roof of earth. The clouds of war are sweeping past and hiding them; but they will shine out again, in due time.

Many of us — most of us, probably — think of progress and improvement as a steady, cumulative, and continuous process which goes on automatically, and all the time, even though we may not see it; which halts for a moment upon hesitating feet, but is never really, or very seriously, interrupted. But that is an obviously mistaken inference for which history gives no warrant. Progress, as Professor Lake has recently pointed out, is a matter of catastrophe and recovery from catastrophe; of long intervals of growth and then a sudden fall from which men rise again with a clearer understanding of their errors and their duties. It always has been so: probably it always will be so. There is sunshine and then shadow; gain which is followed by loss; and then gain once more. It is destruction making way for new fulfillment; ruin followed by recovery; crucifixion leading on to resurrection. For the race is like the individual. It "falls to rise, is baffled to fight better, sleeps to wake."

There is ground, then, as well as room for hope in these days of deep darkness. The young Child was taken away into Egypt all those years ago — but why? Not that He might be lost; but rather that He might be saved. He came again unto His own, to increase in wisdom and stature, and in favor with God and man. And that, doubtless, is the way it is destined once again to be. Every generation has, and must have, its own form of Christianity. For Christianity is shaped and influenced by every advance in knowledge as well as by every failure and calamity of life. In the same way, as some one has said, "Christ becomes the creation of each fresh generation: for each generation creates the world in which it lives." The generations of the past have had many and very different Christs. They have had Christ as God, and Christ as man. They have had the suffering Christ, and the sorrowing Christ, and the sentimental Christ. And in like manner the age that now is dawning will have its Christ — the Christ brought back from the Egypt of to-day. And I incline to think that He will be a social Christ. When this War is over and He begins to reëxtend his sway, He will grow and find new increase along social lines. That is to say, we shall come to think of Him as teaching justice quite as much as mercy, and the rightful use of worldly power as well as simple purity of heart. We shall then see — for the social, serving Christ will make clear to us — that, to have a Christian civilization which is more than a merely surface matter, we must have a new relationship of man with man, of neighbor with neighbor, of one class with another, of employer with employed, of capital with labor, of rich with poor, of nation with nation, and of one race with another. We must build, if we are to build with security and power, on something less superficial than science, less selfish than commerce, and truer than mere trade. We must build on the principle of genuine humanity and the essential kinship of the race.

This is "the Christ that is to be" which the muffled, mournful bells of war are ringing in. This is the Christ which, it is my conviction, will return when the soldiers leave at last the trenches and the thunder of the guns has ceased.

What we want and wait for in the age to come is not more Christians, but truer Christians; not merely more religion, but more real religion. Most of us, in these painful days, are having to reconstruct our faith unless we wish to lose our faith. The old props are, many of them, gone. We cannot think again of human nature exactly as we did; we cannot think of God precisely as we did;

219

nor even of the world we live in just as
we used to do. To have the same faith
we must have deeper faith; to trust at all,
and to believe in goodness, we must have
more ample grounds for confidence than
those which hitherto have seemed sufficient.

And all of this is coming. Out of the
present darkness, if we live, we shall pass
on to a day when we shall celebrate a
truer and completer Christmas. Perhaps
— who knows?—in the years to come
we may revert to the legend and the lesson of that first and glorious Christmas
morning when kings and wise men came
and offered gifts. And, reverting to that
lesson, we shall remember that they did
not offer their gifts to one another: they
presented them to Christ.

Suppose that we should learn to make
such gifts as that. Suppose we should

determine to make the Christmas season what our forefathers desired it to be — a season of deepened faith and not of mere festivities; a season of spiritual life and not of so much levity. Suppose each year we should kneel before the symbol of that Eastern cradle and, taking the most precious things we have, — taking time and thought and energy and wealth and life itself, — we should lay them at the feet of human needs and hopes and high desires. That, it seems to me, would be to celebrate a new birth of the Christ-Spirit, to witness the return of the Child.

When that happens, we ourselves shall be both kings and wise men, and the star of hope will shine before us as we make our way across the desert places of the world. And then at last, not angels unseen in the sky, but men and women as they go about their daily work, will be heard to sing the song of peace on earth, good-will to men; and the song will tell not of promise only, but of fulfillment.

Chapter Ten

UNSHAKEN THINGS

UNSHAKEN THINGS

ONE of the most disturbing and depressing features in the present world-convulsion is the element of grave uncertainty which has been introduced into human life. The old and familiar order has been forcibly upset and far-reaching changes are inevitable. For the moment confusion reigns. The world-adjustment has been overthrown. Accepted standards of international conduct have been openly despised. Dreams of human development have been dethroned and trampled in the mud of unloosed lust and passions that dehumanize. Ideals have been shattered. Human confidence has been shaken to its depths. Christianity has openly been challenged. Religious faith has been made a hideous mockery. At such a time, when confusion and uncertainty prevail, it is the part of wisdom to take thought of such forces as are permanent and unshaken, — unseen, perhaps, and yet, in the midst of widespread chaos, proceeding patiently along their appointed paths.

Some century and a half ago a famous scene was enacted in our colonial history. A sudden "Dark Day," it will be recalled, settled down upon New England. The Provincial Assembly was in session, discussing the great question of constitutional government; when lo, at midday, darkness began to fall. It was all that men could do to see each other's faces. Even the hearts of those stout old Puritans stood still in fear and dumb amazement. " It is the Day of Judgment," some called out. Others cried, "The end has come."

Then one of the Fathers stood up in his place. "Whether it be the Judgment Day, or no, I know not," he said; "but this I do know: it is God's will we save our country and we shall be judged accordingly. I move that the candles be lit and that we go on with our business."

In like manner it is for us to-day to light the candles of faith and hope and reason, and to go on with our business. And our business, as it seems to me, is this: amid the waste and welter of this War, while the surface of society is so confused, to lay hold upon the deeply human things, and to rest upon those mighty spiritual forces which still abide in undiminished strength. " For this word," it is written in the Epistle to the

Hebrews, "yet once more signifieth the removing of those things that are shaken, as of things that are made, that those things which cannot be shaken may remain."

The things which cannot be shaken — those are the things that people love. The things which cannot be shaken — those are the things for which people hunger and thirst. The things which cannot be shaken — those are the things out of which a new order is builded, upon the ruins of an old; by means of which right triumphs over wrong, goodness does away with evil, and life is victor over death.

In the interests of peace, therefore, when it shall have been reached; in the interests of social progress, when it once again shall have been resumed; in the interests of faith, while there is so much

to encourage doubt; in the interests of
the Church whose teachings seemingly
have become of small avail; in the interests of each and all these causes, we
may think together of those things which,
like the Word of God, remain unshaken.
For though " the grass withereth and
the flower fadeth, the Word of our God
shall stand forever."

And a first such thing that I would
name for spiritual comfort, and to restore spiritual confidence, and to establish spiritual guidance, is that thing which
has suffered greatest outrage; which,
because it was neglected, or unrecog-
nized, in former modes of government,
has brought to pass this present world
disaster; but which, none the less, cannot be permanently shaken. It is the
fact of human kinship — the consciousness of a tie that binds the peoples of all

the world together, however they may
have come to be divided, wrenched apart,
and separated by the fact of strife. You
cannot conquer, you cannot permanently
do away with the sense of world-wide
kinship, with the consciousness of a community of hopes and fears, of longings
and endeavors, of faiths and aspirations,
in which all peoples are as one. Human
beings — when the worst and saddest
has been said about them, when their
sins have all been recognized and their
multiform shortcomings have frankly and
fully been confessed — human beings are
intensely human. They are one at heart
even when hand is lifted against hand.
They are one in destiny, however much
destructive forces may for a time divide
them.

You may recall, for instance, a story
that is told of our Civil War: how, on

one occasion, the two hostile forces lay entrenched against each other with just a narrow river flowing in between. Shots were frequently exchanged and threats were hurled from side to side. At the close of the day, when the night shut in, it was the habit of the soldiers to lift up their voices in the respective songs that had come to give expression to their rival causes; and always they strove to drown out one another's music. One night, however, beneath the benediction of the placid stars that shone in the southern sky, as the opposing camps lay in heavy stillness, suddenly a soldier on the Union side began to sing with lyric tenor voice the sweet, familiar strains of " Home, Sweet Home." He sang for a time alone, his voice softened by suppressed emotion. Little by little, however, the words were taken up by comrades, then by those across the stream, till finally the two opposing armies were united in a mighty chorus, chanting together the words that made them one in longing and in sentiment, one in deeply human feelings and desires.

And so to-day, on the bruised and mutilated face of Europe, where hordes of men have clinched and sway together in the fierce embrace of death, there are, even now, more and deeper things which unite the warring millions and the hostile nations than there are, or ever can be, things that divide them. They fight, indeed, for their respective flags which call forth passionate devotion and command a loyalty which sets their hearts aflame with eagerness to do and dare the utmost. But there is one flag flying in their midst, wherever need arises and suffering is felt — there is one flag which

claims allegiance from them all. It shows
no national device. Upon a spotless field
of white, it bears a simple cross of red —
the symbol of humanity. Here is a flag
that does not divide men: it unites them.

I believe, therefore, that when this
War is over, this great unshaken fact of
human kinship is destined to assert itself
and claim such rights of recognition as
never before have been accorded it. In
large part unembodied hitherto, I believe
that this spirit will secure for itself, at
last, some organism which shall mean a
federated world — a United States of
Europe, or of Christendom. That dream
is not a new one although we often think
of it as the product of our own generation. It is a century old at least.

One hundred years ago, after Napoleon, the disturber of the world, had been
beaten into exile, the great Congress of

Vienna was assembled to arrange a peace. The times were such as we may well suppose they will be once again when at length the horrors of this present situation shall have passed away. Representatives of the various nations came together, seeking to settle their disputes. Their prime object was to arrive at terms of peace. And yet, what they talked about was not a temporary truce — a mere mechanical adjustment of long-standing difficulties. No, not that: those men, one hundred years ago, so soon as they had come together, began to talk about a "Federated Europe," and how they might proceed to constitute a "Supreme International Tribunal." The Emperor of Russia, inspired by a sublime idealism, suggested to the Congress that a Holy Alliance should be formed in Europe, to rule according to the sacred principles of Christianity. There was to be a " Council of Great Powers, endowed with the influence, and almost the simplicity, of a single independent State."

Diplomats were amazed at the unworldly scheme. They called it nonsense. But the influence of the Emperor Alexander, who was fired with the high desire to become a " Napoleon of Peace," at length prevailed. Nearly all the nations of Europe actually entered into a solemn compact and signed a form of treaty, in accord with the terms of which they declared themselves " united by the bonds of a true fraternity, pledged to lend aid to each other." Their sole principle of conduct was stated to be a desire " to render mutual service, and to testify by increasing good-will the mutual affection with which they should be animated."

A Confusion of Tongues

And thus the scheme went into operation. For a number of years this Holy Alliance, whose object was international good-will and peace, remained the dominant fact in the affairs of Europe. Further congresses were held in 1818, 1819, 1820, and 1822. Then the Alliance ceased to operate. A Federation of the Powers could not be accomplished, it seemed. And why? Let me remind you why — since the situation has a lesson for the present day. It was because that congress was a congress of monarchs and their representatives only. In it the people had no voice. It was a "Royal Trust" — a "Holding Company" of hereditary rulers who hoped, through combination, to resist the revolutionary movements of the people. The Holy Alliance of one hundred years ago, and the scheme for a United States of Europe, left the actual rulers out of the account. Those rulers are evermore the people: and the people, fundamentally, are one.

A century now has passed and that dream of a Federated World has dawned again. Brighter than before, it forms the bow of promise on the storm-clouds of the world. But if the dream is to come to anything, it will be through recognition of the abiding ties of human kinship, which bind the *peoples*, not alone the rulers, of the nations into one. Autocracies — not peoples — have "got the world into its present fearful mess." And when the world emerges, the people must make an end forever of autocracies. A new world-order is in process of gestation; and when pride of race gives way to consciousness of kind, and the sense of human kinship takes possession of the world, that order will be established.

However, this sense of kinship is not the only element that has abiding power. Amid the world's uncertainties, its causes for anxiety, confusion, sorrow, and dismay, I see another thing that cannot possibly be shaken. Bright and clear it shines out through the smoke of battle and across the tumult of engulfing waters; warm and vitalizing it lends a sacred luster to the stretcher of the ambulance and the cots and corridors of countless hospitals. It is the steadfast, striking, hallowing, consoling fact of human courage; the loyal, self-sacrificing willingness to count life but as something to be laid down and devoted to a great and all-compelling need. It is not displayed on one side more than on another. It is neither French nor German, British nor conspicuously Belgian. It is simply and completely human. What men have to do, they bravely do; what they have to bear is borne with courage and unflinching, undismayed endurance. It always has been so: it is so to-day. The weak display extraordinary strength; the faltering surprise themselves and others by their firmness; the laggards lay down their lives with no counting of the cost; while the sinful and the fallen stand up pure and holy to be counted in the bright array of heroes. It may be, indeed, that we shall think less well of mankind than we used, because this War has come to pass; but, because of it, we shall think much better than we did of individual men and women. For we have come to see the stuff that often lies unused in human nature — the gold that only waits for the refiner's touch to separate it from the base alloy of selfishness and weak indulgence.

When this War is over and has passed into the sad records of history, it will have —in spite of its inhumanities, atrocities, and cruelties — it will have a tale to tell of bravery and endurance, of calm taking of great risks on earth, in air, upon the sea, and underneath the dark and threatening waters, such as never before has been heard. Upon such sacrifices as are being made at present, God Himself must throw the incense of approval. Perhaps in the years to come, because of what the world is nobly bearing up beneath to-day, people will be more patient underneath mere light afflictions; "quicker to put things eternal before things temporal; more simple in their ways; more moderate in their pleasures; more willing to look calmly on the face of death; more conscious of God's presence in the time of. peace."

And yet, while all of this is something to rejoice in and to lend us confidence and comfort, it is likewise something that may well cause us shame. For what have we all been doing? What has the Church been thinking of? Why has not religion used for higher ends these latent, unemployed reserves of human effort and energy? Is it king and country only that can call men to put forth their utmost powers; and not also God and kind? Are we strong only when it comes to kill and conquer, and not equally courageous when it comes to serve and bless? These noble qualities of man- and womanhood, these capacities for holy service, these energies that waited for the call of war to leap full-armed before the world — shall they not some time be enlisted to redeem the world from error and to crown it with content? When religion shall have learned the secret underlying patriotism, and the Church commands what is given gladly to the State, then the kingdom of God will no longer be a golden dream, nor laborers be lacking for the harvest. When the Children of the Light shall have learned to marshal unused human forces as effectively and well as do the Children of the World, then will great hosts of youthful and courageous men and women go forth to overthrow the factors of unrighteousness, and the promises of God will be the performances of man.

But let us look still further and a little higher in our search for elements of life that have abiding power. The qualities that I have spoken of would be comparatively unimportant, they would lack constructive and incentive power, were it not that a third conspicuous thing remains unshaken — not to be swept away, uprooted, or destroyed. It is our confidence in the future : our hope and faith and deep conviction that a new and better order will replace the old; that darkness will give way to light, wrong to rectitude, and error to the truth. Man is an ideal-building, a vision-seeing, a dream-constructing creature. Explain it as you will and account for it as you may, the fact remains that you cannot crush, you cannot kill, you cannot drive from out the heart and mind and conscience of the human race the hope for more ideal conditions; the conviction that a brighter, better, holier state of society can somehow, some time, be constructed. Man feels it, for God has dowered him with certain instincts and desires : man sees it, for God has given him the capacity to look beyond the present and

to see above the threatening and the all-
obscuring clouds : man knows it, for God
has crowned his powers with reason, in-
telligence, and insight. You may shake
the world into confusion; but man rises
up and constructs a new world for himself. You may rend the heavens and dis-
solve the earth into fire-mist, the smoke
of cannon or of poisonous gases; but man
straightway sees a new heaven, and per-
ceives a better earth where the fire of
love is burning and the smoke of incense
rises from chastened hearts and burdened
souls that kneel before the altars of a
truer and a juster dispensation.

When all else fails or has been badly
shaken — when wealth is wasted, plans
are worsted, institutions have been over-
turned and governments upset, with science grievously suborned to dealing death
and devising methods of destruction —

even then there abideth, still unshaken, faith — faith in man and his capacity, with God's ready and unfailing aid, to succeed and to triumph: there abideth hope, whose light can never be extinguished — hope of a better and a happier time to come: there abideth love, the greatest and the most enduring of them all.

Hence it happened that, no sooner was this War declared than busy, earnest, deep-souled thinkers in nearly all — yes, in literally all — the warring nations and the neutral countries set themselves to work and said: " We must marshal all our forces, put machinery in motion and mature plans for making such things in the days to come impossible." The cry was raised at once, and found its way around the world, that this was "a war for the putting down of war." Before a single shot had been fired, while troops were even yet in course of rushing to their places, members of parliament, college presidents, earnest reformers, socialists, and men of science were saying earnestly to one another: "Now is the time to begin a new campaign, to educate opinion and to organize all available human agencies for a lasting peace. Now is the time to shape the future, to set in motion factors and forces that will do away at last with the insensate policies and programmes which have brought the world to this disgraceful pass."

And that is the work which is going on to-day. The candles have been lighted and the Father's business has eagerly been taken up. It is being organized anew, not in America alone, but nearly everywhere; not merely on the parts of professional scheme-makers and avowed peace advocates, but quietly, earnestly, hopefully, in countless bleeding hearts and in lonely widowed homes; in the cabinets of kings and in councils of the common people; in "unions" every-where, whether of labor or of love; not only on the part of men, but earnestly abetted now by women.

Some one has suggested that the task of the century but recently closed was, in large part, a mechanical task — a task of invention, discovery, and adaptation. It was well and nobly and even dramatically performed by engineers and promoters and men of organizing genius. It led to the practical bridging of the ocean; to the conquest of the air; to the hollowing of the mountains; to the harnessing of mighty rivers that the power they contain might be transformed and then transferred to busy factories and quiet homes. Yes, and

247

finally, — the greatest by far of all such things, — it led to the opening of that impressive channel by means of which the East and West have come to be united. All of this — and how much more — has been splendidly and hopefully accomplished.

But it remains for us to do something different and something higher yet. The task which they of the past accomplished was a task of mechanical engineering: ours is a task of social readjustment. It was for them to seek out and develop natural forces: it is for us to regulate and harmonize human forces. They devised and constructed mechanical appliances for vastly increasing human power: it is for us to contrive that this power shall be used for higher ends — for life and not for death, for the common human good and not for selfish, inhuman conquest.

To bring such things about is a matter of ethical engineering. It will require a widespread development of justice, forbearance, and mutual good-will, leading on to radical social readjustment. Nevertheless, it will be accomplished. This will all come to pass, I believe, and at a time not too far distant. And when the new order shall have been achieved, it will be seen to rest upon those unshaken elements in human life of which I have been speaking.

What are we that we should weakly and dishonorably cry that such things cannot be accomplished? What are we that we should grovel in the dust and say that what has always been always must be? If as a race we have learned to move erect as men and, in consequence, no longer move as do the animals, shall we not likewise learn, in time, to live as men

who are members of one human family?
If we have outgrown cannibalism, abol-
ished slavery, put down dueling and
swept away polygamy, is it not probable
that sometime we shall grow ashamed
of war? To doubt it would be less than
human: to deny it would imply denial of
our faith. After all, it is simply a question of the management of our affairs;
and right management merely means an
application of the simplest Christian principles.

Some one has said that "if the so-called
Christian nations were nations of Christians there would be no war." But that,
alas, is only partly true. We have nations
of Christians at the present time: but the
Christian nation is still waiting to be born.
Our trouble is that the Christian religion
has always been too much an individual
matter and not enough a matter of the

social order. We have thought of it as giving rules and presenting high ideals for neighbors in their intercourse with each other, for the rich in their relations with the poor, and for the strong in their obligations toward the weak. We have only just recently begun to think of it as containing guidance for governments in their dealings with each other and for nations in the settlement of their disputes. But until a place shall be prepared in the inn of government and statecraft — some lowly manger where the spirit of the Christ may be born — the hopes and dreams of individual men and women may, at any moment, be overborne, and those principles for which they stand be brought to quick defeat. There is a sense in which a Christian nation is absolutely necessary if we would make possible a nation of Christians. For all of us, inevitably and incessantly, and oftentimes unconsciously, are influenced and guided, shaped and moulded by the system, or the group-idea, of which we find ourselves a part. "A Commonwealth," wrote Milton, years ago when times were dark and strife was general,—"a Commonwealth ought to be but as one huge Christian personage—one mighty growth and stature of an honest man, as big and compact in virtue as in body." And a modern prophet well has said,[1] "The whole creation of government groaneth and travaileth in pain until now, waiting for the manifestation of the Christian life in the modern state."

And so in dark days and in clear, through war and in peace, with a world in conflict or in concord, whether doubt-

[1] F. G. Peabody, *The Christian Life in the Modern World*, p. 193.

ing or believing, whether in trial or in triumph, both while suffering and while serving, alike when working and when at worship, let us hold fast to the things that cannot possibly be shaken. Whatever comes or goes, is lost or found, the fact of human kinship cannot be destroyed; nor can the ties that bind us into one great family be severed. Above the clouds, shine bright and clear the qualities of courage, great endurance, and the eager willingness to serve; while the certain promise of a better future brings light into men's eyes and faces, and gives them heart to greet the unknown with a cheer.

We ourselves are of the present only, and a brief to-morrow. But the forces which are working through us are neither of to-day's nor yesterday's invention. Their one and only source is God. In the mighty march of human progress interruptions may occur; defeats may signally be suffered; a return to lower and less worthy levels may be gloomily endured. But the endless host of human beings, as they make their way across the centuries, do not wander: they are led. God has planted and established certain dominant desires in their hearts, certain soaring aspirations in their souls; and by these hopes and aspirations, instincts and desires, He is leading them upon the march. For a time they may forget, or deny, or suppress these higher instincts. In consequence they go down to the somber, wooded valley of humiliation where the way is lost and the path of destiny and progress becomes entirely obscured. But presently the flame of freedom leaps up again within their souls, the light of understanding shines out within their minds, and they set forth once more to climb great mountains of achievement.

Then they know, for they themselves have helped to prove, that right is evermore superior to might. Then they know that caliber of character is of more importance than caliber of cannon. There are forces at work in this world stronger than bayonets or bullets. Justice carries further, travels faster, thunders with a silent might that makes of small effect the proud inventions and explosive arts of man.

Wherefore, as we view not one nation but all nations, not one people but the human race itself, we can say with fervor as of old: "God is our refuge and strength: a very present help in time of trouble. Therefore will we not fear, though the earth be removed, and though the mountains be carried into the midst of the sea. For the Lord of Hosts is with us and the God of Nations is our refuge."

THE END

BIBLIOLIFE

Old Books Deserve a New Life
www.bibliolife.com

Did you know that you can get most of our titles in our trademark **EasyScript**™ print format? **EasyScript**™ provides readers with a larger than average typeface, for a reading experience that's easier on the eyes.

Did you know that we have an ever-growing collection of books in many languages?

Order online:
www.bibliolife.com/store

Or to exclusively browse our **EasyScript**™ collection:
www.bibliogrande.com

At BiblioLife, we aim to make knowledge more accessible by making thousands of titles available to you – quickly and affordably.

Contact us:
BiblioLife
PO Box 21206
Charleston, SC 29413

Printed in Great Britain
by Amazon

43662908R10152